W9-BLC-230

Beyond Arithmetic

Changing Mathematics in the Elementary Classroom

Jan Mokros

Susan Jo Russell

Karen Economopoulos

DALE SEYMOUR PUBLICATIONS ®

This book was developed at TERC (formerly Technical Education Research Centers). The work was supported in part by National Science Foundation Grant No. MDR-9050210. TERC is a nonprofit company working to improve mathematics and science education. TERC is located at 2067 Massachusetts Avenue, Cambridge, MA 02140.

**This project was supported, in part,
by the**
National Science Foundation
Opinions expressed are those of the authors
and not necessarily those of the Foundation

Editor: Beverly Cory
Production: Barbara Atmore
Design: Nancy Benedict
Cover: Nancy Benedict
Photography: John Guare, Film Cell Photography, Boston

This book is published by Dale Seymour Publications®, an imprint of Addison Wesley Longman, Inc.

Dale Seymour Publications
10 Bank Street
White Plains, NY 10602
Customer Service: 800-872-1100

Copyright © 1995 by Dale Seymour Publications®. All rights reserved. No part of this publication may be reproduced, stored in a retrieval system, or transmitted, in any form or by any means, electronic, mechanical, photo-copying, recording, or otherwise, without the prior written premission of the publisher. Printed in the United States of America.

**DALE
SEYMOUR
PUBLICATIONS®**

Order Number DS21259
ISBN 0-86651-846-0
 7 8 9 10-ML-20 01 00

This book is printed on recycled paper.

CONTENTS

PREFACE

Since the mid-1980s there has been a serious, ongoing attempt to change mathematics education. The National Council of Teachers of Mathematics (NCTM) describes what needs to happen for the effort to be successful:

We need to shift—

- *toward classrooms as mathematical communities—away from classrooms as simply a collection of individuals;*
- *toward logic and mathematical evidence as verification—away from the teacher as the sole authority for right answers;*
- *toward mathematical reasoning—away from merely memorizing procedures;*
- *toward conjecturing, inventing, and problem solving—away from an emphasis on mechanistic answer-finding;*
- *toward connecting mathematics, its ideas, and its applications— away from treating mathematics as a body of isolated concepts and procedures.*

Professional Standards for Teaching Mathematics,
NCTM (1991), p. 3

It is one thing to call for these significant transformations, and quite a different thing to actually implement them. Have teachers been able to make major shifts in the classroom along the lines suggested by NCTM? Read what one teacher says:

The hardest thing is trusting that students will actually become good mathematicians when we follow constructivist principles. It requires a leap of faith ...

In a series of conversations, this teacher talked a great deal about the leap of faith that was required to change the mathematics curriculum and meet the reform goals articulated in the NCTM *Standards.* For her, as for many teachers, this change required refocusing her attention on mathematical thinking, and placing less emphasis on drill and memorization. As she was making this leap, she was trying to interest others in her school. She heard one question repeatedly from her colleagues: "Why should we change?" We were constantly mindful of this same question as we wrote this book. All of us who are now reshaping the mathematics classroom—teachers, curriculum developers, administrators, researchers, teacher educators—must continue to address this question, not only for others, but for ourselves.

The National Council of Teachers of Mathematics calls for a shift in mathematics teaching, as indicated by the quote that opens this preface. In our book, we describe what that shift looks like as it is reflected in curriculum materials, in assessment, and in the everyday workings of the mathematics classroom. We also share our thoughts on issues that seem to be at the core of this shift.

This book is based on the work we have been doing at TERC (formerly Technical Education Research Centers) since 1985, developing curriculum that reflects the NCTM recommendations. Our efforts have included the book *Seeing Fractions* (Corwin, Russell, and Tierney, 1991), the *Used Numbers* units on data analysis for the elementary grades (Russell et al., 1990), and the K–5 mathematics curriculum, *Investigations in Number, Data, and Space* ™ (Russell et al., 1995 and in press). These materials were the collective efforts of a group of classroom teachers, teacher educators, and mathematics education researchers. This team worked directly in classrooms for many thousands of hours, exploring and struggling to understand the complicated interactions of mathematics content, student thinking, teaching strategies, models, materials, and technology. The time we spent in classrooms, as well as the many after-hours discussions with teachers, helped us understand the kinds of questions teachers are grappling with as they change their practice.

We discovered that many, many classroom teachers are experiencing deep dissatisfaction with the mathematics they have been teaching. They have had students who are adept at memorizing facts and procedures, and who have been successful in school and on tests, yet they have watched these same students act frustrated and unhappy when confronted with problems that don't look like the ones they are used to solving. They have seen other students who perform poorly on standardized tests, but who have special mathematical strengths that have not been recognized and developed. They have seen generation after generation of students—from their own to the current generation of students they now teach—leaving school without confidence in their mathematical abilities. They have seen glimmers of mathematical excitement as they try new materials and problems, and they want to know how to expand such scattered, interesting activities into a whole mathematics program that makes sense. They have begun to think that there must be a better way of teaching and learning mathematics, and they are curious about how to do it.

For these readers, we hope that this book can provide a beginning, an occasion for reflection on mathematics teaching and learning, or a source for discussion among colleagues. We begin the book with an inquiry into the reasons that change is needed, and we offer a philosophical framework that links the NCTM goals with what actually happens in classrooms. Next we examine the role of curriculum and consider how it needs to be redefined as a tool for both teacher and student learning. In subsequent chapters, we provide a glimpse of how young students look and sound when they are thinking and reasoning mathematically, address common questions that teachers ask about mathematics reform, describe approaches to assessing mathematical understanding, and discuss the issues teachers face in creating a school climate in which students are active mathematical learners.

This book is not a prescription for change; no one can say exactly how the change process will unfold for each individual. Those of us who are educators, like our students, learn by making our own meaning and our own mistakes. Making changes that are this fundamental will involve considerable time and patience, as well as the willingness to take risks. Yes, there will be days when we fall back on old methods, and days when we wonder whether the new ways of learning are really going to make students better mathematicians. There may even be days when we are tired from thinking so hard about students' mathematical thinking, and we will simply put out the tangrams, the pattern blocks, and the geoboards, and just coast for a few days. But there will be other days when the students make incredible breakthroughs, or construct mathematical strategies so elegant that they take our breath away.

If you are working to change your classroom in accord with the NCTM *Standards*, how will you know when you've made the transformation? While the process is never complete, there will be unmistakable signs that you're getting somewhere. For example, as we walked out of a fourth grade classroom in a neighborhood school recently, we heard the students, on their way to recess, continue to talk about finding the factors of 1000—not about recess, and who has the playground ball, but about mathematics. You'll know you're getting somewhere when the students are doing, thinking, and talking about significant mathematics—beyond providing the answers required by teacher or text. As the classroom is transformed, students will stop asking each other, "What did you get for question 5?" Instead, they will engage in mathematical argument, "Show me how you solved it... I don't think 3 could be a factor of 1000 because it's not a factor of 100... Wait a minute, how can 8 be a factor of 1000?" Mathematics class will begin to last longer and longer, and you—and your students—will sometimes lose track of time. Mathematical charts, writings, drawings, and constructions will start cropping up in every corner and on every wall of the classroom. You will have a parent who drops her child off at school and forgets to leave because she becomes so interested in the math project you are doing. And, perhaps most important, you will find yourself engaged in mathematical thinking of your own. By paying close attention to students' thinking, you will inevitably become intrigued by aspects of the mathematics content that you have not previously pondered deeply. Those "aha!" moments will happen for you, too.

The outcomes just described are more elusive and hard to pin down than scores on standardized achievement tests, but they are real and important outcomes. Students who construct mathematics for themselves are not going to "forget" how to do it over the summer. They will keep trying to make sense out of problems. They will have confidence that mathematics is something they can do for themselves, for their whole lives, for work or for play, in or outside of school. And both you and they will develop a feel for the beauty and power of mathematics:

> *If you do mathematics every day, it seems the most natural thing in the world. If you stop to think about what you are doing and what it means, it seems one of the most mysterious. (Davis and Hersh, 1981, p. 318)*

Acknowledgments

We would like to thank the many people who have regularly talked, constructed, and lived mathematics education with us as we wrote this book. If the book rings true, it is because it is based on what teachers have to say and what we observed in their classrooms. We would especially like to thank the teachers involved year-long in our field tests, including Kathleen O'Connell, Jeanne Wall, Bob Dihlmann, Katie Bloomfield, Angela Philactos, Michele de Silva, Corrine Varon, and Virginia Micciche. These innovative educators were willing to take the risk of trying out the entire *Investigations* curriculum as it was being developed. We also wish to thank those who reviewed the book, including Barbara Fox, Lynne Mayo, Tom Rowan, Anna Suarez, and Margaret McGaffigan.

Although there are three named authors on this book, the work represents the collective wisdom of the talented staff of the *Investigations* project and its sister projects in the Math Center at TERC. We are especially grateful to staff members who took time away from other pressing publication deadlines to read and comment on numerous drafts. Special thanks to Cornelia C. Tierney, who provided teacher-ly advice, no-nonsense feedback, and mathematical wisdom. Beverly Cory, our editor at Dale Seymour, showed enormous patience with our multiple rewrites and unusual insight about how children learn mathematics. Thanks also to the National Science Foundation, which funded our work, and to the staff there who have advocated changes in curriculum and teacher development that are critical to the growth of mathematics reform in the elementary grades.

Finally, we wish to thank all of the children we have done math with, for providing evidence more powerful than all of the research literature combined, that constructivist mathematics education really works.

Jan Mokros
Susan Jo Russell
Karen Economopoulos

CHAPTER I

Teaching Children Mathematics

Do You Remember?

Do you remember how mathematics was taught when you were going to elementary school? If yours was a typical U.S. school, you probably remember pages and pages of practice on the same kind of arithmetic problem. You probably also remember having to memorize many facts, procedures, definitions, formulas. As a child, you probably felt that what was important was getting the right answer to the problems—and doing it quickly, without mistakes. Chances are you always worked on your problems alone, using only pencil and paper. And—if you are like many adults who went through this system—you may now feel that mathematics is not your strength.

The elementary mathematics curriculum that most of us experienced as children has changed very little for decades. Our grandparents, our parents, we ourselves, and our children have encountered basically the same content and approach. Developed to meet the needs of the 19th century, this curriculum has always focused on learning a particular set of procedures for addition, subtraction, multiplication, and division of whole numbers, fractions, and decimals. Claims have been made that the "new math" ushered in a different kind of mathematics during the 1960s. This movement, a direct response to the perceived superiority of the Russians' technological, mathematical, and scientific skills, was based on the premise that the development of mathematics for young children should be grounded in certain logical structures, such as those found in set theory. However, the resulting changes to most mathematics curricula were superficial and short-lived. Children continued to spend the bulk of their time doing arithmetic. The "back to basics" movement, popularized in the 1980s by Hirsch's cultural literacy books (e.g., Hirsch, 1987), emphasized student mastery of a standard set of procedures— the ones we all learned in arithmetic. So, this movement didn't change much about the way mathematics was taught either. In mathematics, we never left the station; there was nothing to go "back" to.

Mathematics in many schools has so long been associated with memorization and practice that we virtually equate school mathematics with learning of this kind. In these schools, the time set aside for mathematics goes something like this: The teacher presents a new kind of problem, carefully goes through the steps to solve it with the class, and does one or two problems together with the whole class. Then students practice many more of these problems by themselves for the rest of the mathematics class and for homework. Mathematics the next day begins with a review of these problems before the teacher presents the next kind of procedure to be learned. Student participation in class consists of giving the answer when called on and being told whether it is right or wrong. Students' comments range from questions about the next steps—"Do I subtract next or bring down?"—to the common and all-purpose "I don't get it!"

The Results of Traditional Mathematics Education

The pedagogical point of view embodied in the traditional curriculum is simple: If you don't get it, do it again and again and again. Practice makes perfect. Only it doesn't. Despite years of training focused on calculation, American children enrolled in traditional mathematics programs have never become mathematically powerful. As results of national and international testing have repeatedly shown, our over-practiced students can apply procedures and formulas when problems are presented in the forms they recognize, but they run into trouble when they have to think. Numerous examples from national and international tests point to our students' weakness in number sense, estimation, and reasoning. For example, students can add up three given prices, but can't choose three items from a menu that total less than $4.00. They can find common denominators to add two fractions, such as $5/6$ and $4/5$, but don't know just by looking that the sum will be a little less than 2.

American students often rank near the bottom in international testing (Stevenson and Stigler, 1992). While a number of factors make it difficult to compare children from different cultures, two striking findings emerge from international comparisons: (1) Students from other countries exhibit better performance on "higher order" mathematical skills such as reasoning, conceptualization, and problem solving, and (2) in many other countries, the mathematics curricula are broader and focus more on problem solving than does the traditional U.S. curriculum.

The age-old mathematics curriculum simply no longer serves the needs of students, schools, or society as a whole. The NCTM, in its *Curriculum and Evaluation Standards for School Mathematics* (1989), calls for a shift from teaching students *procedures* to teaching them to *think and reason* mathematically. This shift is required by the more complex demands of today's society. Employers no longer look for employees who can apply memorized procedures to do rote calculations—everyone's pocket calculator takes care of these quite efficiently. Rather, they look for employees who can face an unfamiliar problem and think of a number of possible strategies to solve it. They look for sound estimation and number sense, skills in spatial visualization, competence in using and interpreting data, and a familiarity with technological tools and processes. This means that students must learn a great deal more mathematics than what we considered sufficient in the past, and that we must make room for more and deeper mathematics in the curriculum. In the past, the elementary curriculum focused almost entirely on paper-and-pencil work with arithmetic, while the study of geometry, data, number theory, and other important aspects of mathematics were relegated to a few special exercises or to chapters that were never reached. The pages in the NCTM *Standards* (1989, pp. 20–21, 70–74) that describe what needs increased and decreased attention in the curriculum must be taken seriously. If students are going to pursue mathematical ideas in depth, we have to make real choices about how they will spend their time in the mathematics curriculum.

What Do We Need to Teach?

The current consensus among mathematics educators and mathematicians is that we can't continue to focus on basic arithmetic, as in traditional curricula, and ignore the much bigger mathematical world that envelops us. A spate of recent books by mathematicians decry Americans' lack of familiarity with large numbers, geometry, percentages, statistics, and logic (Dewdney, 1993; MacNeal, 1994; Paulos, 1988). These books point out that most of us lack even the basic mathematical skills needed to make informed decisions about political candidates, consumer products, and health care. As a result, advertisers and politicians can easily take advantage of our "innumeracy" and present us with information that is at best misleading and at worst downright dangerous.

Our children deserve more from mathematics education. They deserve a curriculum that emphasizes many forms of mathematical thinking and that teaches them to use technological tools. If students are to become powerful and confident users of mathematics, the mathematics curriculum in the elementary school must contain a balance of study in at least four areas: number, statistics or data analysis, geometry, and what we call the mathematics of change. Each of these is described in turn below.

Number

The very first item on the NCTM *Standards* list of what should receive "increased attention" is number sense (NCTM, 1989, p. 20). To have "sense" about number means to understand how numerical quantities are constructed and how they relate to each other. A "numerically literate" person brings a rich web of interconnected knowledge and experience to an encounter with a number such as 5, or 100, or 0.98, or $3/4$. A person with number sense knows how these numbers are related to other numbers, where they fall in the number system, and how they can be transformed into other numbers to make calculation or comparison more manageable.

Consider a practical example of number sense in action:

> I have $1/2$ cup of flour and need $1\,1/4$ cups of flour; how much more flour do I need?

If I have a good sense of these familiar fractions, their magnitudes, and their relationships to each other and to 1, I would be unlikely to use the traditional subtraction algorithm $(1\,1/4 - 1/2)$, which requires that I find common denominators, transform the mixed number into an improper fraction, then subtract. Rather, I immediately "see" that if I needed 1 cup of flour, I would need $^1/_2$ cup more, but I need $^1/_4$ cup more than 1, so in fact I need $^1/_2$ cup *and* $^1/_4$ cup, or $^3/_4$ cup.

Here's another example: Suppose we ask you to add 58 and 57 in your head. Some people will try to use the traditional "carrying" algorithm, but people with good number sense are more likely to do it another way: "Well, 50 and 50, that's 100, and 8 and 7 is 15, so it's 115." Others with good number sense might think: "Both numbers are close to 60. I know 60 and 60 is 120, then I subtract the 5 that I added on, and I get 115." People who use these methods can mentally figure this problem quickly and efficiently. They keep in mind the whole quantities involved rather than breaking them up into meaningless digits ("8 and 7 is 15, put down the 5, carry the 1"). Their calculations are based on sound knowledge of the number system, and they typically have good strategies for estimating and for double-checking for accuracy.

We want students coming out of elementary school to easily calculate two-digit addition and subtraction problems, problems using familiar fractions and decimals, and many other numerical problems mentally—not because they know a memorized procedure, but because they have a deep, rich, connected understanding of how our number system works.

As students grow in their understanding about the number system, they become familiar with very large as well as very small numbers. They get a sense of the size of a number like 3989 by relating it to important "landmarks" in the number system. For example, fourth and fifth graders develop mental images of larger and larger units: 100 is a familiar "landmark" to them, and ten 100's make a thousand, and a hundred 100's make ten thousand. Of course, simply being able to recite this information is not enough. Students must have mental images of how these numbers are built from each other. Once those images are firm, students can use these units to make sense of an even larger number, like 39,989—it is close to 40,000, which is the same as 4 ten thousands.

Students must also become comfortable with small numbers, a task that is in some ways more difficult. Traditionally, students have learned to calculate with fractions and decimals in the elementary grades without necessarily understanding how fractions and decimal numbers represent quantities less than 1. For example, if an athlete scores 5.73 on an event, is her performance better or worse than that of someone who scores 5.8? Many students believe that 5.73 is the better score, because 73 is bigger than 8. These same students may be correctly adding, subtracting, and multiplying with such numbers because they have learned memorized procedures. However, they are not able to apply their knowledge, because they have little idea about what these numbers mean. Finding one's way around the number system and understanding its intricacies is an essential goal of elementary school mathematics. It is clearly a goal that transcends arithmetic.

As students work with numbers, they also think about the characteristics of the numbers themselves. They describe, compare, and classify numbers. For example, a third grade class might investigate odd and even numbers. What makes a number *odd*? How do these numbers behave? When an odd number is added to or subtracted from another odd number, the result is an even number. Why is this true? Students can study many categories of numbers as they move through the elementary grades: primes, factors, and multiples; even and odd numbers; square numbers. As they build their own theories about these numbers and their relationships, students begin to think mathematically and to see and analyze patterns in all the mathematics they do.

Geometry and Measurement

Although much neglected in school, geometric and measuring skills are essential to our everyday lives. Think about how you use these skills when you are reading a map, giving directions to a friend, building a fort with your child, or ordering a window box for your plants. Think about how often you figure out the relationship of shape to area (will the new rug fit properly in the living room?) or to volume (will the leftovers fit in the container you've chosen?). Many people believe that spatial skills are innate—that you are either good at spatial visualization or you aren't. But the truth is, many of us have had very little opportunity in school to work on developing our spatial visualization skills. As in all learning situations, we won't get better at something unless we have enough opportunities to do it.

Much of mathematics and science depends on geometric models

for understanding. When students develop visual models for fractions or for multiplication, they are using geometric relationships to help them think about number. Some students have a very good spatial sense, but have been labeled "not good at math" because they lack strong computational skills. These students can make powerful connections between what is to them the *familiar* spatial world and the more confusing world of number.

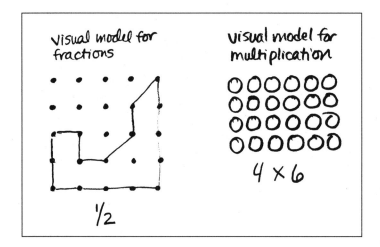

Geometric models can extend and support students' understanding of number.

As students study increasingly sophisticated mathematics and science in school, those who are able to construct and analyze physical and mental models will be at an advantage. An increasing number of jobs are also dependent on these skills. Consider the use of spatial reasoning in the burgeoning field of computer networking, in communications technology, in architecture, and in the development of CAD/CAM (computer-aided design/computer-aided manufacturing) for designing machinery. With the use of computers as modeling tools, we can represent and manipulate 3-D objects on the screen. Translating back and forth between 3-D objects and 2-D representations of those objects—maps, drawings, diagrams, plans—is a central part of many high-tech and skilled-trade vocations. It's not just that more and more jobs require geometric skills; it's also the case that the disproportionately higher-paying jobs demand these skills. By emphasizing geometry in elementary school math, we are giving all our students—not just those who build models and play with computer graphics at home—a wider range of options.

Statistics

It is shocking that Americans learn so little about statistics in school, given the fact that so much of daily life depends upon our being able to interpret and use data. Looking at the morning newspaper one day, for example, we find data on the percentages of children of various ethnic backgrounds enrolled in city schools, with an accompanying statistics-packed article about the disparity in minority enrollment between suburban and city schools. There is also an article comparing the risk of amniocentesis with that of a new procedure, chorionic villi sampling. And, just as there has been nearly every day for a month, there is another article about the relative costs of health care and who would pay those costs under different plans proposed by government officials. In these articles, the reader is expected to interpret data from maps, charts, and graphs; to understand the notion of *median*, and how it differs from *mean*; to make sense of cost-benefit ratios; and to compare different kinds of risks.

Statistics are prevalent in our lives, and critical personal decisions are often dependent on being able to interpret and apply statistical data. But what do we offer in school to help students use and interpret data? Most students learn how to identify the tallest or shortest bar on a graph, how to calculate an average, and how to put data on a line graph, then "connect the dots." But there are serious gaps in their understanding.

Most children and many adults do not know how an average represents the data that it describes. While students can use the add-'em-up-and-divide algorithm for finding the mean, they typically have little idea what this number tells them. When we give students $1.69 as the average price of a bag of chips and ask them to figure out what the prices for 9 different brands might be, they are stumped—they don't have an idea of the prices this average could reflect. When we read about an average in the newspaper, we need to be able to imagine what possible data sets might result in that average. For example, if we read that the average person holds 8 jobs in his or her lifetime, what might this average mean? Does it mean that a large percentage of the population holds, say, 7 to 9 jobs, while smaller percentages hold fewer or more? Or is it the case that the largest percentage holds only 2 or 3 jobs, while another group that holds between 15 and 20 jobs "pulls up" the average? Statistically literate citizens need to ask questions like these and need to integrate information from a variety of sources in order to interpret what the average conveys about the data.

Students must acquire a deep, firsthand understanding of how to ask questions, how to collect data, how to represent these data, and how to make sense of them. Students need to learn to tell the story of the data—the true story, not a misleading simplistic version—and they need to learn how to interpret the statistical stories that they read in the print media and hear on TV. They need to learn about probability if they are to make informed decisions about cigarette smoking, the effects of exercise, or whether they should play the lottery. Of course, many subjective factors, too, affect the decisions we make—but if we don't help students learn some basic statistical ideas, we are sending them into a risky world without the tools they need to evaluate risk.

The Mathematics of Change

Most students do not learn about the mathematics of change until they are in high school or college. During algebra or calculus, students learn to describe and compare rates of growth and to examine patterns of change. In algebra, students begin to learn what a function is. They learn to describe how one variable changes in direct relationship to another—for example, the area of a circle is related to the length of its radius. They make graphs and write equations to describe these functions. In calculus, students learn about more complicated rates of change. They learn that rates of change may not be constant. For example, a baby grows fastest right after it is born, then growth slows down until adolescence, at which point it speeds up. Describing the rate at which something is speeding up or slowing down is an important element of calculus.

Figuring out how quickly something grows or declines is essential in the sciences and social sciences. Despite our mathematics courses, most of us have learned little about the idea of *rate of change*. We are confused by claims and counterclaims about how big something is versus how fast it is growing. For example, during the 1992 presidential debates, Bill Clinton claimed that Arkansas had experienced one of the biggest increases in high school graduation rates of any state in the country. George Bush refuted this, claiming that Arkansas had one of the lowest percentages of high school graduates. Who was right? Both were. Clinton was talking about *rate of change* (and Arkansas had indeed posted impressive gains), whereas Bush was describing the absolute percentages of high school graduates from various states.

Recent research suggests that students should be learning about change many years before they enter high school (Nemirovsky, 1993; Tierney and Nemirovsky, 1991). Even quite young children can and should begin to describe and understand the mathematics of change. As students construct bigger and bigger squares out of tiles, they can describe how the area of the square changes in relation to the increasing length of its side. By keeping track of how tall their bean plants are, students can begin describing in their own words not only the *height* of a graph but its *slope* (the rate at which change occurs): "it suddenly slowed down," "it's gradually growing faster" or "it is growing faster and faster all the time." As elementary grade students examine and talk about change, they are developing important ideas about mathematical representations and relationships.

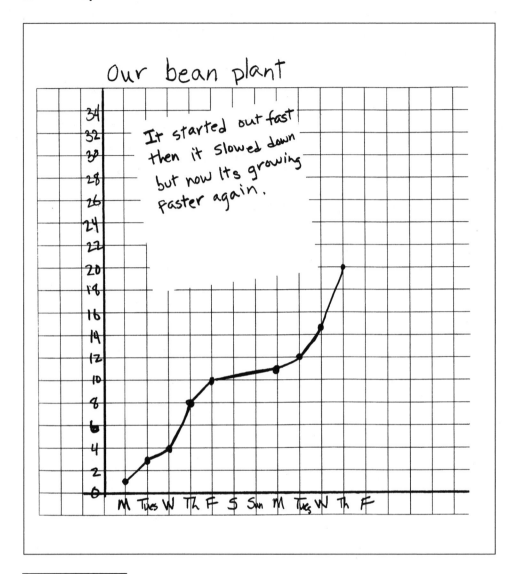

Fourth grade students begin to work with the mathematics of change as they graph plant growth and see how their graph shows changes in the rate of growth.

How Should We Be Teaching All This?

We need to change not just the content of the curriculum, but the whole purpose and pedagogy behind that curriculum, too. In order to learn mathematics, children have to actually do mathematics for themselves rather than learn to follow how someone else does it. This "doing" or constructing of mathematics for oneself is called *constructivism.* Constructivist education, a term that educators are currently using to describe a variety of educational innovations, is not new. It has its roots in Piaget's case studies of how children learn (Piaget and Szeminska, 1965; Piaget and Garcia, 1974). Many of Piaget's studies were about the development of logical and mathematical thought in children. When his insights are applied to mathematics learning, they suggest that children need to develop their own strategies for solving mathematical problems. In the long run, children who develop their own approaches based on mathematical reasoning, rather than relying on memorized procedures, are better, more flexible mathematicians. Children who do not generate their own ways of solving problems are left with a shallow collection of rules and definitions, rather than with real mathematical understanding.

In her book *Mathematical Power,* Ruth Parker (1993) argues that children who consistently learn through constructivist curricula are more mathematically powerful than other children. Similarly, Constance Kamii found that children who developed their own strategies for solving computational problems performed substantially better than children who memorized the recipe or algorithm for doing these problems. Kamii gave the following problem to second graders and fourth graders, asking them to solve it without using pencil and paper: 6 + 53 + 185. She found that only about 23 percent of fourth graders in traditional classrooms could solve this problem, while 45 percent of second graders who had spent the year working out their own strategies for solving numerical problems solved it accurately (Kamii, Lewis, and Livingston, 1993). The evidence increasingly supports the position that students who learn to think mathematically, rather than to simply apply mathematical recipes, understand mathematical ideas much better.

Mathematics is a way of approaching a problem by using one's own logic and powers of observation. It is not a recipe for problem solving, but rather a collection of ways of using reasoning, models, evidence, examples, and counterexamples to discover meaningful patterns in numbers, in 2-D and 3-D space, and in data. Like science, mathematics has standards of proof: An argument must be supported by evidence, and conclusions must be logically derived.

Students of any age can and should learn how to argue mathematically, both orally and in writing. Consider the following argument from Hanna, a second grader who was asked to determine whether you could land exactly on 100 if you counted by fives:

> "Well, first I went 5, 10, 15, 20, 25 like we learned, and I did land on 100. So it works. But Jamie [her partner] didn't get it because maybe I was going too fast. So I got out the play nickels and I put them down and I said SLOWLY 5, 10, 15, 20 each time. And I got to 100. But then, you know, Jamie said "How much do you think we have?" At first I didn't know. So we did 5, 10, 15 again. But in the middle of it, I just knew it was going to be $1.00. Because counting by fives is like adding it all up. You land on the place that is the same as how much you have altogether."

Hanna has proved that skip counting by fives is the same process as repeated addition. She realizes that each time she counts, she is actually adding and accumulating another five. Her proof is based on a combination of logic, work with manipulatives, and use of a number pattern.

As we observe more and more "Hannas" in action, we support ever more strongly the conclusion of the Mathematical Sciences Education Board:

> More than most other school subjects, mathematics offers special opportunities for children to learn the power of thought as distinct from the power of authority. This is a very important lesson to learn, an essential step in the emergence of independent thinking. (National Research Council, 1989, p. 4)

Hanna solved the problem correctly, but in her classroom, her mathematical work is not finished when she has a solution. She assumes that part of her job, as a mathematical thinker, is to be able to demonstrate and explain her solution and to convince someone else of its soundness. It is a giant leap for educators to begin teaching mathematics as "the power of thought" rather than "the power of facts." Making this fundamental leap is essential if we want our students to be mathematically literate.

CHAPTER 2

The Jobs of a Mathematics Curriculum

The traditional mathematics curriculum offers to teachers the tools for teaching a set of procedures, definitions, and "facts." It offers them a sequence of topics, a clear delineation of the procedure for each kind of problem, and lots and lots of problems of each type. A curriculum that is essentially a book of sequenced problems is no longer adequate to meet the needs of today's students and teachers. As an educator, you have the right to demand a great deal more from a mathematics curriculum.

What Is a Good Mathematics Curriculum?

A good mathematics curriculum provides a coherent set of investigations that allow all students at each grade level to explore important mathematical ideas in the use of number, data, geometry, and the mathematics of change. These investigations focus on the mathematics that we now understand to be especially important, such as learning about the number system; understanding the relationships among operations; describing, graphing, and reasoning about data; finding and analyzing patterns; measuring and estimating; and visualizing and describing objects in two-dimensional and three-dimensional space. In a good curriculum, the student activities have been thoroughly tested in a variety of classrooms representing a diverse student population. A good curriculum is structured so that all students have the opportunity to work with significant mathematical ideas; to build confidence, knowledge, and skills; and to discuss, represent, and write about their work.

Just as important as providing good mathematics for students, the curriculum of today must provide support for teachers. The teacher's role in the mathematics classroom is a complex and demanding one. It requires that teachers understand a great deal about mathematics content, teaching approaches, models and materials, and children's thinking. Much of this understanding must be developed on the job as teachers observe and listen carefully to their students. To support teachers in this difficult role, the curriculum has the responsibility to help teachers learn *while* they teach.

While writing this book, we and our colleagues at TERC are deeply engaged in designing a constructivist mathematics curriculum for elementary schools *(Investigations in Number, Data, and Space™, 1995 and in press)*. We base our work on the belief that a mathematics curriculum has several jobs that it must accomplish:

1. providing good problems for students
2. articulating a clear set of goals for mathematics learning
3. focusing on mathematical thinking
4. providing both coherence and depth of mathematics content
5. supporting teacher learning
6. connecting all students with mathematics

The First Job: Providing Good Problems

Which of the following is a good mathematical problem?

a. $42 \times 37 = ?$

b. Nora has 42 people coming to her party. She wants to give each of them a bag of 37 peanuts. How many peanuts does she need to buy?

c. Each year the fifth grade takes a trip to Washington, DC. They have a car wash to raise money to pay for their expenses. This year there are 42 students in the fifth grade. The bus fare and lunch will cost $37 per student. How much money do they need to raise to pay for the expenses of all the students?

d. None of the above.

e. All of the above.

If you like, think about your response to this question before reading further.

Of course, the very problem we have just presented is not itself a good problem. That is, it is not possible to respond adequately to this question in a multiple-choice format. As soon as you began thinking about this question, you probably began to consider circumstances and contexts: Who are the students? Where did the problem come from? How does it relate to the other mathematics the students are doing? What is the teacher's goal?

You might have thought that problem *b*, about Nora and the peanuts, sounds kind of silly. For one thing, no one buys peanuts by counting individual peanuts, and why on earth would she want bags of 37 peanuts? However, your opinion might change when you find out that this is a problem created by a third grade student in response to the question, "What problem situation might go with the equation 42 × 37 = 1554?" The student is perfectly aware that the problem is a silly one—she intended it to be silly—but is nevertheless showing very well her grasp of multiplication as a situation involving equal groups.

Many of you might criticize problem *a* as lacking context and therefore not constituting a "real problem." Your opinion might change if you observed a mathematics lesson in a fifth grade classroom, listening to students discuss and compare their mental strategies for solving this problem:

> *"I figured out that it would be about 1500, because forty 40's would be 1600, but the answer is going to be about three 40's less than that."*

> *"It's exactly 1554—here's how I did it. It's the same as multiplying 42 by 40, then subtracting three of them. So—ten 42's is 420. Double that to get 840. Then you double that, so it's 1680. Then you have to subtract three 42's. Two 40's down from 1680 is 1600, then another 40 off is 1560, then subtract 6 more. So it's 1554."*

In a classroom where students are expected to develop and share strategies based on good number sense, problem *a* can be a terrific problem.

Perhaps you initially liked problem *c*, because it is a problem that seems to be grounded in a real context. Yet if you learned that this problem was just one on a page of ten such problems designed for student practice of two-digit multiplication, you might wonder whether students pay any attention to the "real" context at all and whether for some students—say, those who had never traveled far from home—the context might actually get in the way.

In designing or selecting mathematical problems, one goal should be to maximize the potential of the precious little time each classroom spends on mathematics. There are many potentially "good" problems. However, there are also many levels at which a problem is or is not "good," with criteria ranging from the practical to the affective to the mathematical. If students love the activity but do not learn any mathematics from it, then it is not a good mathematics problem. If the students are engaged in significant mathematics but the activity is not manageable in an average classroom situation, then it is not a good mathematics problem. If the potential mathematics is superb but students aren't interested in the activity, then it is not a good mathematics problem.

Curriculum developers and teachers looking for good problems will ask questions like these:

- Does solving this problem lead to work with significant mathematical ideas and relationships?

- Does the activity lead students to consider important mathematical ideas that reach beyond the particular result?

- Are there different ways into this problem, so that students with different strengths, needs, and experiences will be able to engage with some aspects of the problem?

- Is the problem interesting to a wide range of students?

- As students become involved in the problem, are they grabbed by the mathematics in the problem, or do nonmathematical aspects of the investigation tend to take center stage?

- Do the constraints of the problem provide enough direction and structure without overly restricting the ways in which students might think about the problem?

- Does the problem lead to satisfying closure for the students? Do they feel they've arrived somewhere when they are finished?

- Does the problem tend to support writing about, talking about, constructing, and representing student ideas?

- Are the necessary materials available and manageable?

The question about "grabbing" students with the mathematics in the problem is particularly interesting. Watch students at work, and you'll see that good "grabbing" problems sometimes start with purely mathematical questions, while other times the mathematics is initially tangential to other questions that children have. For example, imagine groups of kindergarten and first grade students working with data about the number of people in their families. Their initial interest may be in their own families and the particular people in them. But as they count and represent their families, they begin to show a lot of interest in the relationships among these quantities:

"I have 4 people, you have 6."

"You have 2 more people than I do, but I have 1 more than Kim."

"When our new baby is born, I'll have the same number as you!"

These same young students might be intrigued by an exploration that started in a purely numerical context:

"Look how we made 6 three different ways, see, 1 red and 5 blue, 2 red and 4 blue, and 3 and 3."

In the first case, the students' own experiences provide a meaningful context for counting and comparing. In the second example, the students become fascinated with the color and numerical patterns that they can make in their cube stacks. In both instances, students are focusing on important mathematics.

However, the context can overwhelm the mathematics, so that students are clearly busy and interested but are not learning much. For example, when we first worked with fourth and fifth graders on developing opinion surveys, we found that most students could develop simple questions and graph their results in a bar graph, but they had little to say about their data when they were finished. They reported that most people liked a certain television show or preferred a particular brand of sneaker, but their thinking did not go much deeper than that. In fact, we were distressed to notice that these older students were designing the same kind of surveys, making the same kind of graphs, and drawing the same kind of conclusions as students we observed in primary grades. Not much mathematics learning was going on here.

What mathematical ideas about representing categorical data were important for these older students? How could we redesign our activities to connect students with these ideas? After some reflection and more classroom testing, we realized that these students needed to discover alternative ways of representing their data so that they could see more aspects of their data. For example, if they did a survey on what occupations interested their classmates, they came up with a few people in each individual occupation—1 person wants to be a computer programmer, 2 people want to be teachers, 2 want to be doctors, 3 people want to be rock stars, 1 wants to be a movie star, 1 a singer, and 1 wants to be a veterinarian—and nothing much to report beyond that. But, if they thought about larger categories, they began to get different views of their data. For example:

> *"About a quarter of our class wants to help sick people or animals."*

> *"Most of us want to be in a profession where we could be a star."*

These children were capable of synthesizing data and making generalizations when a potentially good problem was connected to important mathematical ideas.

A good problem is not simply a mathematically creative idea in the mind of the developer; it is a problem that works in action. To identify such problems, curriculum developers work closely with a few teachers over time, observing class sessions and taking careful notes. They talk to the students as they work to understand new mathematical ideas. They talk with the teachers about what their students are learning and about the practical aspects of implementing the activities. This process repeats several times as the curriculum units are developed and revised. It is time- and labor-intensive, but it ensures that mathematical problems meet the multiple criteria for feasibility, interest, and mathematical integrity.

The Second Job: Choosing
Goals for Mathematics Learning

Whether or not a problem is a good one is strongly affected by the mathematical goal of the activity. Defining a goal helps both curriculum designers and classroom teachers make decisions about the context for a problem, how it is presented, what students are asked to do, how they are expected to do it, and how their solutions are considered. The NCTM *Standards* are challenging us to shift the goals of our mathematics curriculum. Because we can carry out only so many goals and still do a good job, choices have to be made. If we are to truly shift our emphasis to problem solving and reasoning, we must focus on the difficult task of getting students to think, explain, justify, and demonstrate.

A curriculum whose primary goal is the development of mathematical thinking will look very different from a curriculum that is aimed at teaching students procedures, and this difference will show up in the classroom. When the curricular goals involve flawless execution of the standard borrowing and carrying algorithms for addition and subtraction, much class time will be spent on mastering these processes, with concomitantly less emphasis on mathematical thinking. When a primary goal is the development of sound understanding of the number system, on the other hand, students will spend much of their math time putting together and pulling apart different numbers as they explore the relationships among them. Even if both classrooms include manipulative materials and small-group work, the different goals will radically affect what students do, how they do it, and what behavior is valued in the classroom.

Many curriculum developers start with the goal, or at least the presupposition, of "covering" all the usual mathematical topics and subtopics, perhaps even covering them in a particular sequence. This starting place, with its implicit set of goals, no longer makes sense. Instead, curricular goals should emerge from three places: (1) significant mathematics, (2) students' actual mathematical understanding, and (3) the assumption that students learn best by doing mathematics for themselves. The interplay of these three factors is demonstrated by what we learned about third-graders and number.

To develop goals for learning about number in grades 3 and 4 of *Investigations,* we began by working with students to find out what they already knew about the number system. We soon found that third graders' knowledge of numbers in the hundreds was not very deep. They could tell us that the number 342 was composed of "3 hundreds, 4 tens, and 2 ones." But they could not make much use of what they were able to recite and really didn't have much knowledge at all about this number's magnitude or its relationship to other numbers. That is, they did not know that 342 is ten less than 352, ten more than 332, or a hundred more than 242. Some did not even know that 342 is between 300 and 350, and few could tell us easily how far 342 is from 400 or 1000.

We learned that something important was missing from students' understanding of the number system. After further reflection, reading, and discussions with other mathematics educators, we concluded that students lacked a deep understanding of anchor points in the number system, which we began referring to as "landmark numbers." These numbers, such as 100, 200, 500, and 1000—are referents from which we build much of our knowledge about the number system. The students we observed were mostly operating as if one number was the same as any other. There was nothing for them to hold on to, nothing to use as an intermediate point in figuring out how far one number was from another, or in determining how many times one number fit into another. We decided that learning about these landmarks and their place in the number system should be a central goal for students.

With this goal in mind, it made sense to focus student work on taking apart and putting together 100 and multiples of 100, using 100's to build other numbers, and learning about how numbers such as 20, 25, and 50 are related to 100 and multiples of 100. This would also lead to considerable work with multiplication and division as students answered questions such as, "How many 40's are there in 400? in 800? in 520?" But our investigations would be guided by a goal to build students' understanding of the number system, not by a focus on teaching particular procedures for multiplying and dividing. If the students could develop a good sense of factors and multiples, they would have a grasp of the relationships among these numbers and be able to draw on this knowledge to solve problems.

Translated into specifics, these became the major goals in the third-grade unit on "landmark" numbers:

- Developing familiarity with the factors of 100, an important landmark in our number system, and their relationships to 100 (for example, that there are twenty 5's in 100 and five 20's in 100).

- Using knowledge about factors of 100 to understand the structure of multiples of 100 (if there are four 25's in 100, there are twelve 25's in 300).

- Developing strategies to solve problems in multiplication and division situations by using knowledge of factors and multiples.

To reach these goals, we designed activities that involve students in exploring factors through counting and grouping in a variety of contexts: using 100 charts, building with interlocking cubes, and dividing amounts of money. They also solve problems in which they use their knowledge of factors and multiples in contexts that range from baking cookies to dividing a school population into classrooms. They create a 100 chart and ultimately a 1000 chart so that they can see the relationships between these numbers and their factors.

Changing our goals in teaching mathematics lies at the heart of the mathematics reform movement. Good curricula must draw on current research and extensive work in the classroom to choose goals that reflect our best knowledge about student understanding of mathematics. It is part of the job of new curricula to help educators redefine their goals for the teaching of mathematics and to provide stimulating mathematical investigations that help students reach these goals.

The Third Job: Focusing on Mathematical Thinking

CALVIN AND HOBBES by Bill Watterson

CALVIN AND HOBBES copyright 1994 Watterson. Reprinted with permission of **UNIVERSAL PRESS SYNDICATE.** All rights reserved.

This cartoon is a sad commentary on the relationship of yesterday's and today's children to mathematics. What a wonderful problem! Here is exactly what we want students to be able to do—pose their own problems about aspects of their world that are of interest to them. Yet, as soon as it becomes clear to Calvin that the way into the problem is through a series of mathematical procedures, he loses interest. For him, mathematics is invented by someone else. It does not occur to him that he could think through this problem for himself.

Our goals for the mathematics curriculum are not only about *what we teach* but about *how students learn.* If overall goals for students are to support mathematical problem solving and reasoning, then the expectations in the classroom must focus on thinking. As the teaching of mathematics becomes the teaching of mathematical thinking, the whole nature of classroom work and discourse changes. Students are expected to describe and represent their approaches to problems. Talking, writing, drawing, and constructing become central parts of classroom activity. Teachers' questions focus on reasoning, evidence, and strategies, rather than on answers:

> How many 20's make 100? How do you know? Who can prove it a different way? How many 2's make 100? How do you know? Who has a different way to explain the solution? (Russell and Rubin, 1995, p. 34)

An emphasis on mathematical thinking should be at the center of a mathematics curriculum. What does this really mean?

- Children are expected to think for themselves about the mathematics they do, rather than simply applying learned procedures and definitions. This often means that students work on only one or two problems during a class session—or perhaps are immersed in a single investigation for several sessions.

- Children have multiple ways to enter a mathematical problem. There is no single approved way. Because children have several ways of solving a problem, they can double-check their results by using more than one approach. They compare approaches with each other and engage in serious discussions about differences in their strategies and their results.

- Children learn to keep track of their mathematical strategies and communicate them in ways that make sense to themselves and others.

- Interpreting an answer, figuring out whether it is reasonable or not, and explaining why it does or does not make sense is an integral part of mathematical problem solving.

Problem solving is the core of a constructivist curriculum. Children of all ages can do powerful mathematical problem solving when they are encouraged to grapple with challenging problems. The following example shows the depth of young children's mathematical thinking.

Looking around the circle of kindergarten students, the teacher dramatically posed this question:

> "How many eyes are there in our classroom?"

This question completely captivated the 5- and 6-year-olds. After discussing the problem briefly, students conferred with their partners and designed their plans for data collection and counting. They were encouraged to use whatever tools they needed to solve the problem, including calculators, buttons, cubes, drawings, and the display of photographs of all the members of the class.

The question was not easy; students who wanted to count actual people found it impossible to get everyone to sit still, and keeping track of who had been counted was a problem that not everyone solved the first time around.

As they worked on this problem over an entire math class session, students made representations to show how they solved it. They knew that when they returned to the group the next day, they would have a "math conference," at which point each pair would explain their strategies.

When the conference began, the teacher asked Shanti and Joshua to explain how they solved the eye problem. The students showed their chart with two buttons pasted next to each person's name, then proceeded to count by twos until they arrived at 50, the total number of eyes for the students. Their work is shown on the next page.

Shanti ⊕⊕
Joshua ⊕⊕
Cortney ⊕ ⊕
    Elias ⊕⊕
Nicole ⊕⊕
    Alex ⊕ ⊕
Selia ⊕⊕

    Chris ⊕⊕
Victoria ⊕⊕
    Nora ⊕⊕

Robin ⊕⊕
D.J. ⊕⊕
Lance ⊕⊕
Jason ⊕⊕
    Larisa ⊕⊕
Heather ⊕⊕
    Tuong ⊕⊕
Michelle ⊕⊕
    Kymberly ⊕⊕
    Jared ⊕⊕

Timothy ⊕⊕
    Sean ⊕ ⊕
Tai ⊕⊕
    Lisa ⊕⊕

Brianna ⊕ ⊕

Partners are encouraged to design their own plans for data collection and counting. To figure out "how many eyes in the classroom," Shanti and Joshua made a class list, copying the names from the display of class pictures. They used buttons to represent each classmate's eyes.

Kathy challenged this solution, because it didn't include the teacher. Kathy and her partner Abdulah had done the problem a different way:

> "We counted 25 kids, and 1 teacher, which is 26. If we each had one eye, it would be 26, but we have 2 eyes so you have to go 26 plus 26."

The teacher encouraged Kathy to explain how they did such a difficult calculation.

"We knew 26 to start, then we counted 27, 28, 29, 30. And kept on going. I counted and Abdulah tried to keep track. But it was too hard, so we got out some cubes and made piles of 26. Then we counted them all up."

Almost as an afterthought, Abdulah said that they got 52 eyes.

Shanti said that it must be right, because she and Joshua got 50 with just the kids, then you'd say "51, 52" to add on the teacher.

In this kindergarten class, students are dealing with mathematical content that sounds familiar to primary teachers. They are counting and adding. But the way they are thinking and learning emphasizes proof, justification, representation, and communication. In our view, one of the most important jobs of the mathematics curriculum is not only to encourage students to think, but to help them think like mathematicians. Mathematicians savor problems and consider them from many different angles. They value an elegant solution. They take time to solve problems and to mull over the problems with their colleagues. As they work on a problem, they keep track of where they've been and represent their problem symbolically and through the use of their own invented representations. The solving of a problem often opens up a flurry of communication between mathematicians, some of it verbal, some in writing. These same thinking and problem-solving processes are at the heart of a good curriculum for elementary school students.

The Fourth Job: Providing Both Coherence and Depth

One of the hardest jobs of a curriculum is to provide students an appropriate variety of mathematical content, while still presenting that content in depth and providing coherence over the course of a year or several years. Many new curricula are addressing the issue of depth by structuring a year-long curriculum as a set of *modules* or *units*.

The traditional curriculum is fragmented; it covers many topics, often changing topics every two pages. Students rarely have a chance to explore any topic in depth or to develop a solid understanding of some of the big ideas in an area of mathematics content. In contrast, a *unit* pulls together a number of mathematical investigations related to a focal content area such as measurement, data analysis, fractions, multiplication, geometric shapes, or the number system. A unit is *not* a collection of activities to be pulled apart and used singly, even though an individual activity from a unit might "work" by itself. The purpose of a unit is to link separate activities together in such a way that students can explore a few important, related mathematical ideas through different problems and contexts that build on each other. Being engaged in the entire unit, having time to investigate the same ideas in several contexts, and spending time thinking, writing, and discussing these ideas is what allows students to make the ideas their own.

Designing any curriculum involves making choices about what is included and what is excluded in a particular unit or at a particular grade level. These choices are difficult to make. Curriculum developers and classroom teachers alike are pushed and pulled by all kinds of expectations old and new—the "shoulds" ring in our heads about what we "ought" to make sure second graders encounter. However, if we are to give students and teachers the opportunity to explore *some* mathematical ideas in depth, we can't possibly present *all* the worthwhile mathematics that might be included at a particular grade level. We better serve students by helping them study *some* mathematics in depth than by trying to cover the entire range of possible mathematical topics.

Teachers and curriculum developers need to begin taking a longer-term view of the development of significant mathematical ideas. Students should revisit the big ideas of the elementary curriculum year after year, from different perspectives. Consider the idea that fractions are equal parts of a whole. What is *one-half?* It is a fraction of a pizza, or of the distance from my house to yours, or of a group of people. *Half* is the result of dividing one cookie among two people, or it is one out of every two cookies, or it is the number of cookies in one of two equal piles. *Half* the money in my pocket is a different amount than *half* the money in your pocket.

This difficult idea needs to be addressed over many years as students' thinking about one-half becomes deeper and more complex.

Second graders might compare shapes and find out that a half a rectangle can be a triangle or another rectangle. In third grade, students might use fractions to help make "fair shares": How would you divide 15 cookies fairly among 6 people? And in fourth grade, students might use fractions to describe data they've collected: 14 out of the 26 students were born in this state, and that's a little more than half of our class. Through experiences like these, students develop a model of $1/2$, and of its relationship to other fractions and to whole numbers, that works in a variety of situations.

The many connections within mathematics support this longer-term approach to curriculum development. For example, a particular year's work might not include an extended study of *area*. If, however, the students use *arrays* to explore multiplication (that is, 4 rows of 6 cubes representing 4×6), these ideas are closely linked to using square units to describe the size of a two-dimensional shape. The following year, when the students make scale drawings of their classroom as part of a measurement unit, they will already be familiar with the idea of using square units to describe the area of a surface. As we watch students engage in significant mathematical investigations, we become much more adept at anticipating and highlighting the connections students can make to other mathematical content.

To shape an elementary curriculum that has depth and coherence, we can also look to several new models of middle-school curricula that embody the directions defined by the NCTM *Standards*. What do these curriculum developers expect of students entering the middle grades? First, they expect students to have a strong foundation in whole-number concepts and operations. They expect them to have a firm grounding in the structure of the base ten number system and excellent skills in estimation and mental computation. On the other hand, they do *not* expect students to be able to do difficult computation with fractions and decimals, multidigit multiplication, or long division—topics that have historically taken a high percentage of the time devoted to mathematics in grades 3–5 (Glenda Lappan, a principal investigator on *The Connected Mathematics Project*, and Glenn Kleiman, principal investigator on *Seeing and Thinking Mathematically*, personal communications, June 1994).

The implication is that elementary curricula need to provide students time to work with ideas about number in depth, so that they build a large repertoire of knowledge about number relationships and operations. Whole-number computation is an area in which the elementary mathematics curriculum needs to be slowed down and deepened. Rather than being hurried into complex computation, students need time to develop strategies based on numerical reasoning. Rather than computing with larger and larger numbers, students need many experiences with the relative magnitudes of ones, tens, hundreds, thousands, and millions. Rather than memorizing algorithms for multiplying and dividing fractions, students need to learn how to interpret and compare fractions.

Beyond a solid understanding of number, innovative middle grades and high school curricula expect students to come in with basic knowledge about data and geometry. So, during each elementary school year, students need significant experiences with collecting, graphing, and interpreting real data. These experiences must become more complex over the elementary grades, so that by fifth grade, students are not simply designing the same kinds of simple surveys and bar graphs they developed in first and second grade. Similarly, students need to work with geometry each year to develop spatial visualization skills, to construct and represent objects in two-dimensional and three-dimensional space, to measure and describe using a variety of units, and to connect their understanding of geometry and number. Finally, students need to study the mathematics of growth and change during elementary school as they develop ideas about functional relationships and rate of change that provide the foundation for algebra and calculus.

In putting together "the big picture," the important thing for both teachers and curriculum developers to remember is that there is no single *right way* to make the choices about content and focus at each grade level. In our development process, we drew on research, the work of middle grade and high school curriculum developers, discussions with teachers, and observations of students doing mathematics to inform our judgments about the critical mathematics for students at each grade level. We have learned that if we listen to anxieties about "coverage," we will again end up with a fragmented curriculum that does not support the development of mathematical thinking. We must instead engage students in selected topics in mathematics, give them time to pursue these topics in depth, challenge them to think hard about the mathematics they are doing, and support them in making connections among different areas of mathematical content.

The Fifth Job: Supporting Teacher Learning

With the publication of the NCTM *Curriculum and Evaluation Standards* (1989), a renewed interest in mathematics has emerged among elementary teachers. As they participate in professional development at their schools, take courses at local universities, attend conferences, or learn about the NCTM *Standards,* many become dissatisfied with the way they have been teaching mathematics. Some teachers, excited about the shift in language arts to the reading of whole texts and to writing as a process, wonder if there couldn't be a parallel and equally exciting change in mathematics. They want mathematics to have a depth and spark that it has not had, and they have begun searching for materials and ideas that might support mathematical reasoning, problem solving, and communication (Ohanian, 1992).

This experience is often frustrating. While it might be easy to find good, individual activities, it is extremely difficult to put together a curriculum that has continuity and coherence from the assortment of collected activities, supplementary materials, and ideas gleaned from in-service workshops. Students might be excited by a particular activity, but it is unclear how to support and extend their interest. As one teacher said, "I really got fired up about using pattern blocks to teach fractions, and we worked on this for several weeks, but then I didn't know where to go, so I went back to the textbook."

More workshops and more courses are not necessarily the answer. Rather, elementary teachers need a new kind of curriculum—one that not only provides good investigations for students, but that enables the teachers themselves to grow as professionals, to learn more about mathematics content and more about how students learn mathematics.

This sort of mathematics curriculum and the teacher will work together in partnership. Both teachers and the curriculum bring to this partnership important contributions. Here is what the curriculum can do to support the partnership:

- Provide notes and explanations about important mathematical ideas, why they are important, and how students might effectively work with these ideas.

- Demonstrate, through the use of classroom examples, how classroom discussions involving mathematical problem solving are guided by the teacher.

- Show how other teachers' students have become involved in different investigations, and make suggestions about what to look for and listen for as students undertake these investigations.

- Provide a variety of ways of assessing students' learning, as well as guidelines for how to interpret students' understanding.

- Show how mathematical ideas in various parts of the curriculum are connected, and suggest ways of helping students discover these connections.

- Give as many specific examples as possible of ways that teachers can support student learning through listening and questioning.

The role of teachers in this partnership is to connect the particularity of their classroom and their students to the investigations presented by the curriculum. Teachers need to listen to their students, figure out how they are understanding various concepts, and make decisions about where to put more or less emphasis. It is up to teachers to use the feedback they are getting from student assessments to plan the next steps they will take in the classroom. Do students need more experiences with counting by twos before they start counting by fives? Are some students needing even more basic work, while others are ready to move on to much more challenging work? If so, how can group work be adjusted to accommodate these different needs? One of the most important things we learn from working in classrooms is that every group is quite different, and no curriculum can be scripted to suit all. While teachers can use the curriculum as a guide, they will still need to make decisions based on what they learn from working with their own students.

Perhaps the most important written material in a constructivist curriculum is the teacher's book. Students at the elementary grade levels do not need a textbook; they need to be actively engaged with mathematics, with their peers, and with manipulative materials. On the other hand, teachers *do* need a book that not only includes directions for all students activities, but also provides ways for teachers to learn more about mathematics teaching and learning.

Seen in this way, each mathematics unit can be a minicourse for teachers about a particular domain of mathematics. As teachers use new curriculum units from one year to the next, they will continue to learn more mathematics and more about their students' mathematical thinking. What they learn from watching and listening to their students will illuminate what they read in the teacher book, while what they read there will enable them to better listen and watch. As teachers and students learn and grow together, the material continues to grow with them.

The Sixth Job: Connecting All Students with Mathematics

If there is one thing we can be sure about in schools, it is that within one classroom, the range of students' needs, interests, strengths, and experiences is *always* a wide one. As any teacher knows, even classes at the same grade level in the same school can vary a great deal from year to year. There is often as much variation within a classroom as between classes or grade levels. We suspect that when teachers use a constructivist curriculum, the wide variation in students' interests, skills, and backgrounds is more exposed than it is with traditional curriculum. When students use their own approaches to solving problems, it becomes clear that these approaches are diverse and cannot be neatly ranked on a continuum from low to high.

To do its job, a curriculum needs to serve the wide range of skills and talents that a teacher routinely encounters. It must meet the needs of children who have traditionally been labeled "good at math," those who are quick and facile with computations. These students are often placed in accelerated classes where they are encouraged to cover more material at a faster rate. We believe that this form of acceleration can be damaging to students in the same way that painting by numbers is. Yes, you can teach students to paint by numbers, and they may indeed make a technically sound product. But take that next step—ask "accelerated" students to create their own pictures—and you'll find that many of them cannot. Painting by numbers only prepared them to do more painting by numbers, not to actually paint. It's the same with math. Rushing through single-, then double-, then triple-digit multiplication with students who pick up the facts quickly is not providing good instruction. The faster students are at picking up traditional arithmetic, the fewer opportunities they may have to explore mathematics in depth.

A curriculum must also serve those students who have been labeled "slow at math." Traditional curricula are often torturously slowed down for children in remedial programs. These students are subjected to endless repetition of the same boring procedures, under the belief that if teachers repeat the procedures over and over, at some point a lightbulb will go on and the children will finally understand the mathematics (or at least be able to do it.)

A sixth grade acquaintance of ours, who had considerable trouble with memorization, spent three years being drilled on the multiplication tables. During those years, she never got an opportunity to do anything else in mathematics. Even more distressing, at the end of that period her teachers concluded that she was simply one of those kids who are "not good at math." They never saw her considerable mathematical talent—this was a student with remarkable spatial skills, who was making elaborate architectural drawings as early as second grade. Rather than discovering and capitalizing on her geometric skills, her curriculum and teachers led her to believe she could never master mathematics.

An important job of a curriculum is to meet the needs of children with different abilities *without* resorting to ability groupings. Research has shown that tracking can seriously compromise students' confidence in their learning (Wheelock, 1992). To avoid the inequities of tracking, Wheelock and other researchers recommend "high-level curriculum for heterogeneous groups." By this, they mean the following:

> *Untracking demands innovations in curriculum and instruction to offer all students the learning experiences often reserved for the "high" students. These innovations organize learning around investigation and discussion of meaningful problems, are multidimensional, and involve students in hands-on activities that offer diverse routes to knowledge. (Wheelock, 1992, p. 149)*

Any curriculum of today must also serve students from diverse cultural and linguistic backgrounds. A mathematics curriculum, like a language arts or social studies curriculum, should nurture an appreciation for diversity; it can even capitalize on this diversity in the problems it poses. When students are asked to gather data about their families or to find out what games are played in their neighborhood, they connect mathematics to the reality of their own cultural experiences. In class, they then enrich the program for everyone by sharing their diverse backgrounds. For example, a Japanese student we worked with in a field-test classroom became very engaged in an activity comparing the number of school days in different countries. He had a firsthand basis for comparing the quality as well as quantity of school days in two countries, and his perspective was valued by his classmates.

To accommodate the diversity of English-language abilities, mathematics classes and curriculum need to provide connections between spoken and written language, with many nonverbal supports, including numbers, symbols, drawings, models, manipulatives, gestures, demonstrations. Children who speak different languages will have an easier time understanding the mathematics when they connect the spoken sounds "thirty-one" with, for example, the number of buttons on a page, or the number they get on the calculator when they add the number of pockets for all the children in their group, or the number that results from $50 - 19$. By doing collaborative mathematical investigations involving models and manipulatives, students who are learning English can connect what they are *doing* to solve a problem with what is being *said* about solving the problem. It is the job of the curriculum to make these connections explicit.

The Curriculum Belongs to the Teacher

We've told you now what we believe a good mathematics curriculum is and does. Perhaps just as important is what it is *not:* It is not a prescription to be followed to the letter. It is not cast in stone; it is not the final word. If a curriculum is doing its job, it does not restrain creative and dedicated teachers, but provides the content and guidance that supports them in doing their best teaching.

Teachers who have found traditional curricula inadequate may be tempted to reject all mathematics curricula. How can a written curriculum anticipate the diverse ways in which their unique class of students approaches mathematics? Of course, it can never totally match all the needs, interests, and experiences of students in any particular classroom. But if it meets the criteria we have discussed in this chapter, it can go a long way toward supporting the teacher's and students' mathematical work. As one teacher recently wrote about her use of a constructivist curriculum: "The units fit my philosophy and style. By using them I can concentrate on my teaching and the children's learning, instead of on curriculum design. It's taken me a while to feel that this is OK. Now I think it's not only OK, but very important. It allows me to focus my energies and attention."

A curriculum that works is a curriculum forever in process. If the curriculum works as it should, in every classroom where it is used, that teacher and those students will make it their own in ways that the curriculum authors could not possibly have anticipated.

CHAPTER 3

A Look Into the Classroom

Mathematics classrooms are changing. With the publication of *Curriculum and Evaluation Standards for School Mathematics* (NCTM, 1989) the mathematics education community has come together around new objectives for the elementary classroom. In the constructivist mathematics class today, students work together, consider their own reasoning and the reasoning of others, and communicate about mathematics in writing and by using pictures, diagrams, and models. They carry out a small number of problems thoughtfully during a class session, or perhaps work on a single problem for one or several sessions. They use more than one strategy to double-check, and they use blocks, cubes, measuring tools, calculators and a variety of other materials to help them solve problems.

To demonstrate, this chapter invites the reader into a third grade classroom. On this particular day, the math session is organized as Choice Time—students have the option of working with their partners on any of several different activities. In one activity choice, we see the students and their teacher engaged in a challenging problem—how a number giving the total height of six third graders can be decomposed into six reasonable heights. (The following scenario is based on actual work undertaken by a third grade class during the *Investigations* field tests.)

Math Time in a Third-Grade Classroom

The teacher begins this morning's math work by reminding students where they have been and where they are going:

> *"For the last few days you have been working on strategies for adding and subtracting. Today you'll continue working on ways to combine numbers to come up with a total.*

> *"For most of today's class, you and your partner should continue playing the game Close to 100 and keep working on finding the heights of six third graders. At the end of today's Choice Time, we'll have a discussion about the heights problem. So if you and your partner haven't finished that activity yet, that would be a good place for you to begin today.*

"Who has an idea about what activity they would like to start with today?"

Students turn to their partners and discuss which activity they will begin with. Many pairs consult their math folders, looking through their work from previous days and checking over their list of activity choices. Hands go up as partners agree on their first choice. Pair by pair, the teacher asks them their choice and sends them off to work. Occasionally there is a quick discussion about the activity choice.

> *"We know where we're going today," announces Elena. "We need to work on the heights problem. Yesterday we measured lots of kids, but we didn't have a chance to figure out which combination of six heights would total 318 inches."*
>
> *"That shouldn't be too hard," adds her partner Jess. "We have lots of information about the heights of the kids in our class— some kids were even 50 inches tall, so that will be easy to add."*
>
> *"Sounds good!" the teacher tells them. "Remember that you don't have to use only the heights of kids in our class. You can use any height that you think is reasonable for a third grader. I'll check in with you in a few minutes to see how you're doing."*

The teacher then continues reviewing plans with the remaining pairs of students.

The Class at Work

During the previous three math classes, these third graders have been working on a set of activities that involve combining and comparing numbers. Today, after the brief introduction from their teacher, the students quickly get down to work. Some students head for the math supplies that are stored in shoe boxes covered with brightly colored paper and arranged on a bookshelf. They collect a calculator, measuring tools, and paper. Other students clear off their desks, arranged in clusters of four, or find another area of the classroom where they can work. In a short time, most students are busily engaged in their chosen activity. It's clear from the way students organize themselves, collect their materials, and settle into the class session that these routines are familiar and well established.

The two girls, Elena and her partner Jess, walk over to one corner of the classroom where they join three other pairs of students. Some are measuring each other's height, and some are recording height information on the wall chart. Other students are using calculators to figure out how the heights of six third graders can add up to 318 inches. One pair, Pete and Jamal, are in the middle of this problem, which they began during yesterday's class:

> *"OK," says Jamal, "if we have two kids at 50 inches and two kids at 53 inches, that's 206 inches. Now, if we want to get to 318, we just . . . "*
>
> *"Yeah, we just subtract 206 from 318. I'll do that." On his calculator, Pete enters 318, the minus sign, 206, and the equals key. "There, it's . . ."*
>
> *"It's 112!" announces Jamal, who hasn't looked at the calculator.*
>
> *"Yeah! It is!" says Pete, staring at his calculator. "Hey, you beat the calculator!"*
>
> *"Well, I just counted up. See, if you add 100, that's 306. Then 10 more is 316, plus 2—that's 112 in all."*
>
> *"But 112 inches is too much," groans Pete. "That's a giant!"*
>
> *"Well," says Jamal thoughtfully, "but it's for two people, so what if we split it in half?"*

Pete agrees and begins to divide 112 by 2 on his calculator. "What did you get?" he asks Jamal.

> *"56. See, half of 100 is 50, then half of 12 is six."*
>
> *"OK—so two people at 56 inches. We're done! But wait—we'd better check and see if anyone in our class is 56 inches. That's pretty tall."*
>
> *Jamal grins at Pete. "I AM 56 inches! I'm pretty tall for a third grader."*
>
> *"So it works," says Pete. "I think we're done with this one."*

As Pete and Jamal finish and choose another problem to work on, Elena and her partner are still working on the same problem. The notes on their paper indicate that they are able to come up with six numbers that total 318, but one of the numbers they are including is not a reasonable height. Their teacher joins the girls as they try to explain their problem. On their paper they have written:

    46 in.   48 in.   49 in.   50 in.   50 in.   75 in.

> *"We're kind of stuck," Elena explains to the teacher. "Most of these numbers are the right height for third graders. Like, Yoshi is 46 inches tall, and I am 48 inches tall, and Kaiya is 49 inches tall. But we have 75 as one of our numbers, and no one in our class is THAT tall—but that's how many more inches we needed to get to 318."*

> *"Hmm, that's an interesting problem. What made you decide to use these heights?"*

> *"Well," explains Jess, who up until this point has been pretty quiet, "we wanted to use kids from our class, so we started out trying to use 50 inches, because 50's are easy to add, and I'm 50 inches tall. So we made two people be 50 inches—that's 100. Then we used Kaiya's height because that's 49 inches and that's close to 50. So with these three people we had 150—no, 149 inches, that's less than half of 318. And then we . . . um, then we just started adding numbers from the list of people's heights, and we ended up needing a 75, but that's too tall for a third grader."*

Their teacher thinks for a moment and then comments:

> *"So, it seems like you had a plan for the first three people. Try going back to that point. You said that 149 was less than half of 318. How much less than 318 is 149 inches, and does that help you think about this problem in a different way? Don't forget that you don't necessarily have to use only the heights of people in our class."*

Elena writes on their paper:

    150 + 150 = 300   300 + 18 = 318   150 + 18 = 168
    168 + 1 = 169

"There. 169 is what's left," says Elena, dropping her pencil on her desk. "We have to make 3 people be 169 inches tall."

"Try some more 50's," suggests Jess. " . . . Oh no, I take that back. 50, 100, 150—that's the right number of people, but not enough inches."

"Wait, I get it. Let's just add some inches onto the 50's until we get to 169. OK, if we add 2 inches to each, that's 150, 2, 4, 6 . . . 156. Nope, not enough."

"Try 3 inches," suggests Jess. "That's 150, 3, 6, 9, 159. Nope."

"Wait, if we try 5 inches, that will give us 150, 155, 160, 165. We're still 4 inches short."

"Well, don't add them to the 55's, because those people are getting too tall. Add it on to the 49 . . . that will make it 53."

By this time Elena and Jess's paper is full of numbers. They decide to go back and circle their final six heights: 50, 50, 53, 55, 55, 55. They then transfer these numbers to their recording sheet.

As Elena and Jess continue working on this problem, some of their classmates are finishing up their first choices. Elena and Jess barely notice. In this classroom, it is not uncommon for students to work on one math problem for an extended period of time, just as they might work on writing a story or conducting a science experiment. A few at a time, partners move to a different activity, putting away one set of materials in exchange for a new set.

Checking In Around the Class

Meanwhile, the teacher continues to check in with pairs. She moves about the classroom purposefully, carrying with her a clipboard on which she has listed the names of six children that she wants to make sure she talks with by the end of class. In addition to notes on these six students, she has jotted down several other observations that she has made this morning about the students in her class. She writes each note on a sticky label, similar to an address label. Later she will transfer each of these labels to the pertinent student's page in her main notebook. For now, though, these quick notes can help the teacher plan questions for the discussion at the end of today's class, as well as formulate plans for tomorrow and decide which individuals she needs to work with during tomorrow's Choice Time.

The teacher glances at the clock and announces to her students that in 5 minutes, they will be gathering on the rug to discuss the heights problem.

> *"Come prepared to share your strategies for how you solved this problem. Bring any work with you that might help other people understand your thinking. And don't forget to clean up your area before the discussion."*

The Follow-Up Discussion

Once the class has gathered together, discussion begins with the teacher asking students about the problem:

> *"Lots of you had different strategies for working on the third grade heights problem. What was it that made this a challenging problem?"*

> *"Well, you couldn't use just any six numbers, which we tried to at first. You had to use numbers that made sense. Like a third grader couldn't be 80 inches tall. So you had to figure that out first."*

> *"I thought keeping track of all the numbers was hard. You needed a system."*

> *"The part I thought was tricky was having to balance the numbers. Like the first time we added up six numbers, it was over 318 inches. So then we had to make some of the numbers smaller, but not too small."*

The teacher picks up on each of these comments.

> *"So, deciding which numbers were reasonable, keeping track of your work, and balancing the numbers made this a challenging problem. Hmmm, balancing the numbers. Let's think about that for a minute. Do any of you have an example of a way to solve this problem where you had to balance the numbers? Elena and Jess, you worked on this problem for a long time."*

> *"We sure did!" moans Jess. "We got really stuck because we wanted all the heights to be from kids in our class. But what we ended up doing was choosing three kids, adding up their heights,*

and then figuring out how much more we needed."

Elena adds, "We started with three 50's because 50's are easy. Then we just kept adding the same amount of inches to each 50 until we got close to 169—which was how much more we needed." Elena holds up their paper, which is covered with numbers—some circled—and equations.

"Then," continues Jess, "we needed 4 more inches, so we added that to our lowest height, and that gave us 318."

They write their numbers on the board:

50   50   53   55   55   55

As Elena and Jess are explaining their strategy, the teacher makes notes on her clipboard, based partly on what she hears, partly on what she sees on their paper, and partly on what she overheard as the two girls worked on the problem. Next to Elena's name, she takes note of the counting-up strategy that Elena used to figure the difference between 318 and 149. She also makes a note of Jess's use of 50 as an important landmark number in adding large numbers:

"Elena and Jess, don't forget to staple that page of work to your recording sheet, because it really shows someone else how you thought about this problem. I'm curious, how would you double-check your answer to be sure that these heights add up to 318 inches?"

"50's, I'd use 50's. See there are 50, 100, 150, 200, 250, 300. Then just add the rest: 5, 10, 15, and 3 is 18. Yup, 50's work every time!" comments Jess confidently as she puts her papers in her folder.

The discussion continues with other students sharing their strategies. Soon there are five combinations of heights on the chalkboard, all totaling 318 inches. Many students notice that most of the numbers are in the 50's. The teacher, picking up on the fact that many students eventually used a few numbers as "anchors," focuses the last part of the discussion with the following question:

"How would knowing Jess's and David's height help you to solve this problem?"

By asking this, she gets the students to think about how they might use additional information to solve the problem.

Talking Mathematics

The discussion between partners as they solved the heights problem *and* the classroom discussion about students' strategies are two key components of mathematics class. Talking about the mathematics they are doing gives students the chance to clarify their thinking. Quite often, students are able to refine their strategies and ideas by telling someone about them and by responding to questions from their peers. It is not unusual for students to make new discoveries about a problem or concept in the midst of discussing it.

In much the same way that many teachers encourage students to share a story they have written in order to gather feedback and ideas from their peers, so should we encourage students to share the mathematical problems they are working on (NCTM, 1991). Rethinking, rewriting, and refining are as important to the process of solving problems and understanding mathematics as they are to the writing process (Corwin and Reinhardt, 1989).

How, then, does a teacher support mathematical discussion in a busy classroom? Because it is more difficult to speak and listen in a large group, students need other contexts for discussing problems. Sometimes this means turning to their partner and talking about the problem for one or two minutes; sometimes it means discussing a problem in a small group of four or five people. Other times, it means presenting a piece of work to the whole class, perhaps using an overhead projector and transparency to show the work they have done. In each situation, students are explaining and listening to one another.

Teachers play an important role in promoting effective discussion: We serve as a primary audience for our students. By clearly wanting to hear many different ideas, by asking questions that promote thinking, and by listening carefully and with interest to what students are saying, we model the important components of a good discussion. We show how to listen, question, reason, and be engaged in a discussion. We demonstrate how to be an effective audience for another's work.

Writing Mathematics

Just as students should be engaged in frequent mathematical discussions, so too should they be encouraged to explain their problem-solving strategies in writing and with pictures and diagrams (Countryman, 1992). Writing about how they solved a problem is a challenging task, but one that is certainly worth the investment. As with any writing assignment, many students will need support and encouragement as they begin to find ways of communicating their ideas and thinking on paper. For most, writing as part of math class will be a new experience.

Once again, students need their teacher and their peers as an audience for their work and as models for communicating mathematical ideas on paper. Being an audience for our students' writing means that we have to provide feedback often, through questions, in order to help students communicate their thinking more clearly and in greater detail. When students read their writing aloud, or when we review student work ourselves, our job is to point out those ideas that clearly convey student thinking and those that need more detail and development.

Even the very youngest students can be encouraged to represent their problem-solving strategies on paper. Consider one first grader's account of how many objects she counted, as shown in the illustration. Initially, Shayna's writing said simply "I have 30." When prompted to record how she figured that out, she added "$5 + 5 + 5 + 5 + 5 + 5 = 30$," indicating how she used groups of 5 to count her set of objects.

Questions and prompts like "How did you solve the problem?" or "Why did you choose to count by fives?" may help extend students' thinking. When students are having a difficult time getting started with their writing, it is often helpful if they first explain orally—to the teacher or a partner—how they solved a problem, then put their spoken words into writing.

Name _Shayna_   Date _March 7_

How Many Sticks?

I have → 30!!

I have
5 + 5 + 5
+ 5 + 5 + 5 = 30

Part of "writing mathematics" is learning to record not just the answer, but also the strategy used to get it.

Some teachers are able to communicate to their students, "I care about what you write (or say); I value your ideas, and I can learn from what you write." These teachers find that they can expect high-quality written work from their students. In this sense, the writing task is seen as much more than just another assignment to turn in; it becomes a real back-and-forth exchange between student and teacher about the student's ideas and strategies.

Expectations and Goals for Our Students

The student's role in mathematics class should be an active one. In the classroom we have just portrayed, students are actively engaged in solving mathematical problems and thinking critically about their approaches. They communicate their ideas and strategies to each other, either in writing or in discussions, as they work to develop an understanding of important concepts. By encouraging students to approach mathematical problems in whatever ways make sense to them and by offering students a variety of tools to work with, we immediately open up the world of mathematical problem solving to a wider range of students. The message that *all* students can do challenging mathematics is an important one.

Besides expecting every single student in the class to do challenging mathematics, we need to communicate to the students that we expect them to *collaborate.* Working together productively and really listening to each other is something that students will learn to do over time. They will need practice at this, particularly if they are accustomed to thinking about small group time as just another opportunity to socialize. If we give students lots of chances to discuss problems in both small and large groups, then they come to identify this as a time when important mathematics is done. The teacher also needs to give students clear goals for this work, such as arriving at a solution that they will show to the entire class or writing about how they solved the problem. Teachers and students need to share the expectation that group work will involve productive discussions.

Mathematical problem solving should be at the same time rigorous and accessible. In the reformed classroom, students are expected to think, talk, and write mathematically. They will learn from others and at the same time contribute to the learning of others. Following are some of our expectations for students who use a constructivist curriculum:

☞ **Students spend time and effort working on nonroutine mathematical problems.**

Students will be doing fewer problems than they have in the past, but they are expected to become deeply engaged with these problems.

These are not problems that they can do while watching TV. The process is more like writing a story, working on a challenging puzzle, or figuring out how to do a difficult tumbling stunt. The process involves trying different ways of solving a problem (some of them likely to be dead ends), going as far as they can with this method, and changing the method if it doesn't work. Students need to understand that getting wrong answers is an important part of the process. In fact, wrong answers often give us clues about which directions to try next.

With nonroutine problems, students should expect "messiness." There may be different paths to a solution, and there may be several different good solutions to a problem. Consequently, students need to be patient, take risks, and try a few different approaches. Real mathematicians often spend months or even years on a single problem. This is not what we expect from student mathematicians, but they do need to learn that problems are to be savored, reconsidered, and lived with for awhile. Doing mathematics often means rough drafts, tentativeness, challenge, and hard work.

☞ **Students learn to generate and use their own strategies, rather than memorized algorithms, to solve problems.**

We expect students to think their way through a problem, rather than rely on a memorized procedure or recipe for solving it. They need to make sense of a problem, understand what it means, and come up with their own methods for solving it. The important thing is that students learn to generate strategies that help them make headway. They may use different strategies for dealing with different pieces of the same problem. In all likelihood, they will learn to use a few different strategies for solving the same problem.

Notice the different and effective approaches employed by the students who worked on the heights problem. Elena and Jess broke the problem into parts, and first tried to find out how tall three third graders would be. While this was an effective strategy for beginning the problem, it became more complicated as they got closer to the goal of 318 inches. They knew that they needed to end up with reasonable heights, and this constraint meant switching strategies and working with a "base" number of 50 from which they could make individual adjustments. Pete and Jamal started to use the same strategy as Elena and Jess (that is, adding up a few heights and seeing how close they were). However, when Pete and Jamal bumped up against the problem of finding "reasonable" heights that also work mathematically, they employed division (112÷2) as their finishing strategy. Both pairs of children showed flexibility, as well as tenacity, in solving this problem.

☞ **Students share strategies with each other.**

Students need to do mathematics collaboratively. By this, we do not mean that they are assigned specified roles, as they are in many cooperative learning approaches. Rather, all students in the group participate in joint problem solving. By sharing strategies, asking questions, and demonstrating how they think, students not only present varied perspectives but also clarify their own thinking and learning. When students are asked to consider a strategy different from their own, they must view the problem from a new perspective. Though students do not always understand or agree with the strategy, they nonetheless come to see that there may be more than one way to arrive at a solution. By sharing different approaches, students experience mathematical problems not as rigid, one-dimensional problems to be solved, but as flexible, multifaceted situations to be explored.

Think about what the students learned from working together on the heights problem. Remember Jamal's explanation to Pete for how he figured out the difference between 318 and 206? "I just counted up. If you add 100 to 206 that's 306, and then 10 more is 316, plus 2 is 318." Jamal's knowledge of landmark numbers like 100 and his ability to think flexibly about the problem, figuring the difference between 318 and 206 by counting up from 206, were possibly new ways of thinking for Pete, who was also amazed that his partner could beat the calculator. And in the other pair, when Jess totaled the six heights by first calculating the 50's and then adding what was left, she was demonstrating how it's often easier to break numbers apart into more familiar components and then add from left to right. For some of her classmates, this may have been a new piece of information to consider, or it may have verified their own similar strategy. In any case, students expanded their experience with this problem while explaining their own thinking to others.

☞ **Students learn to document and keep track of their strategies.**

As students work on problem solving, they need to find ways to keep track of their work and their thinking. By doing so, they will be able to reflect on it, double-check it, change it, and share it with others. Consider Elena and Jess's work with the heights problem. On their recording sheet, they had written the possible heights of six third graders totaling 318 inches, but most of their thinking and processing of the problem was evidenced on a separate page where they "kept track" of the possibilities. Elena's equations ($150 + 150 = 300$; $300 + 18 = 318$; $150 + 18 = 168$, and $168 + 1 = 169$) express how she "counted on" to figure out the difference between 149 and 318. The fact that she was able to keep track of how much she was adding ($150 + 18 + 1 = 169$) suggests a strong grasp of the quantities and process she was using. Without this type of documentation, it would have been clear that Elena and Jess had found a possible solution to the problem, but how they thought about the problem would not have been evident.

☞ **Students become confident learners of mathematics.**

One of our key objectives should be for students to enjoy and appreciate mathematics. If students are to use mathematics, to continue studying mathematics beyond minimum requirements, and to maintain a lifelong curiosity about mathematics, they must come out of school with a sense of mastery of its power and appreciation for its beauty. In a classroom where a variety of strategies and approaches are not only encouraged but valued and respected, students gain a sense of empowerment and are more willing to take risks. This risk taking will in turn launch them into new levels of learning and understanding.

This critical affective component of mathematical learning in the elementary school is closely tied to the view of mathematics that we communicate to students. How students feel about themselves as mathematical learners has many implications for their future success in the field. By creating a safe and respectful environment, students will feel more confident in taking risks. By using all solutions, even incorrect ones, as opportunities to learn rather than measures of success or failure, we send an important message to our students: Take the risk, allow yourself to be challenged, and trust that you have many tools and colleagues to help you with a problem. To effectively send this message, we have to believe and convey that all students can be powerful mathematical learners.

The Teacher's Role

Many teachers experience a significant change in their role when assuming a constructivist approach to mathematics teaching and learning. We hear comments like these:

> *"I feel like less of a director and more of a facilitator."*
>
> *"I had to become a listener instead of an explainer."*

This shifting role can sometimes feel liberating, other times confusing and threatening.

In a classroom where students work together, use manipulative materials, and discuss and write about their thinking, the teacher's role is critical, but may be unfamiliar. Where teachers were once in the front of the room, they are now on the side or in the back. Where they were once sitting at a desk while students worked in their seats, they are now circulating around to small groups, listening in on conversations, observing students as they work, and asking questions to stimulate and extend thinking. Where teachers were once teaching, or more precisely *telling* students *how* to do a problem, they are now encouraging students to make sense out of problems in their own ways. Where there was once *one way* to do a problem, there are now *many ways* to solve a problem.

The reformed curriculum requires both a shift in the teacher's role and a shift in the teacher's view of what's important about mathematics learning. While changes might seem easy on the surface, consider for a moment what it means *not to teach* a third grader the conventional algorithm for subtracting two 2-digit numbers. We may have to alter the types of mathematical work they do. We will definitely have to alter the ways that we measure what our students know and adjust the ways in which we report on students' progress. This includes redefining what we want students to learn. The teacher's role in a constructivist classroom is multifaceted and involves being a decision maker, a leader, a learner, and a researcher.

The Teacher As Decision Maker

Using their observations of students and conversations with them, teachers need to make decisions about how the mathematics curriculum will unfold in their classrooms. Sometimes these decisions may involve changing the numbers to adapt a problem, making it more accessible or more challenging to particular students. Other decisions involve setting the pace of an investigation—choosing to go more slowly through certain sessions, or to add additional sessions. Some decisions concern how students will work together, perhaps in pairs or small groups. In order for teachers to feel confident about the decisions they make, they must become both careful listeners and close observers.

The Teacher As Mathematical Leader

Teachers must be the mathematical leaders for the students in their classrooms. What questions can I ask to push my students further into the mathematics? Which aspect of this discussion should I follow up on? Which part of that student's written explanation needs further explanation? In order to answer these questions, we need to have a sense of where our students are mathematically and where they need to go next.

This doesn't require knowing everything there is to know about all areas of mathematics; it simply means being able to extract the important mathematical ideas that are being expressed in a classroom. In a whole-class discussion, it's not enough to have each group of students share their strategies. After listening to all perspectives, the teacher can step in to highlight an important mathematical idea—not by identifying it as "the right way" or "the best way" to solve a problem, but by asking questions that encourage students to focus on an important aspect of the problem, to consider a conjecture that someone has made, or to compare the strategies presented by different students. For example, in the class discussion of the heights problem, the teacher never told her students how to solve the problem, but instead listened to the variety of strategies that were shared. Then, with a question, she focused the students on two key ideas: "balancing" the numbers, and using an anchor number as a starting point. In doing so, she highlighted mathematical strategies that were particularly effective.

As teachers become more comfortable with leading discussions and observing students as they work, they become more attuned to seizing the mathematical moments that occur in their classroom. The ongoing orchestration of mathematical work demands lots of on-the-spot thinking. It means "deciding when to provide information, when to clarify an issue, when to model, when to lead, and when to let a student struggle with difficulty" (NCTM, 1991, p. 55).

The Teacher As Learner

Like their students, teachers should be closely engaged with the mathematics that is being taught. Many teachers using a new curriculum will be learning or relearning some of the mathematics right along with their students. As important as it is to encourage risk taking in students, teachers too need to feel comfortable taking the risk of learning mathematics with the class and being willing to work through a problem without necessarily knowing the right answer.

One teacher we know spoke quite candidly with her students about being a learner in the area of three-dimensional geometry. She built models with her students and struggled alongside them to see objects from different perspectives. In doing so, she opened herself up as a learner to her students. Her students responded with earnest and articulate explanations of their thinking. Our advice is to plunge into any unfamiliar mathematics problems yourself. Talk mathematics with your colleagues and with your students. Think of how powerful it is for a student to hear the teacher say, "That's an interesting problem you found. Let's try to figure it out together."

The Teacher As Researcher

When teachers ask questions like "Why do you think that?" and "Can you explain your strategy to me?" they begin to collect important information about how children learn and what they understand about a particular concept or problem. This information often influences a teacher's decisions about where to go next with a concept, or how to support students in the learning process. In this respect, teachers are researchers in their own classrooms. They are gathering information, considering it, attempting to make sense out of it, and then using it as the basis for instructional decisions. You saw this happening in the vignette of the third grade classroom. As the teacher moved about the classroom, she jotted down notes about what her students were doing and how they were thinking. These observations helped her structure and guide the discussion about comparing numbers and finding total amounts.

The teacher as researcher is a new role for many of us, a role that adds depth and direction to our teaching (Duckworth, 1987). In a constructivist classroom, teachers have many opportunities for this sort of research. Some teachers may be interested in following an idea through the entire school year. They might examine, for example, how students develop the need for negative numbers, or how they construct graphs from tables of data they have collected, or how they develop ideas about volume. Being curious, asking questions, and really listening to and observing students rewards teachers with new information that can, quite simply, help them be better teachers.

Getting Started: "Where Do I Begin?"

Change, even when fueled by desire and interest, can feel overwhelming. Finding a place to start may not be as simple or obvious as it seems. Research confirms again and again that the most effective and long-lasting changes in teaching occur gradually, over time (Schifter and Fosnot, 1993; Ball, 1988). *Time* and *support* are two key elements in helping teachers make changes in their classrooms. Support can take various forms. One form is written—curriculum materials that provide a suitable structure and sequence of activities, inspiring confidence that the important mathematical ideas are being addressed.

Another form of support is human. Just as we encourage students to work together and share ideas, we encourage teachers to get together, with partners or in small groups, to share classroom experiences. Teachers' initial experiences while changing mathematics in the classroom will probably be mixed; some class sessions will go well, and others may not go anywhere. By exchanging these experiences, teachers can gain insight into what made some class sessions work and others be more frustrating.

Assuming that the materials are available and some form of collegial support is in place, what does a teacher do during the first days and weeks of school to establish the right sort of mathematical environment? Before beginning, a teacher should consider these issues:

- How will I organize and arrange the physical space so that it promotes exploration and interaction?

- How can I best encourage students to use our materials and tools effectively and responsibly?

- How will I create a mathematical culture in my classroom?

Setting Up the Classroom

How a classroom is arranged and organized can significantly affect how students and teachers work within it. The physical space must work for the teacher while also promoting mathematical thinking and communication. With desks or tables arranged in clusters, students can easily work together in pairs or small groups and can move around the classroom easily. Some classrooms, especially at the primary grades, may not need desks at all; activity centers with small tables and ready access to materials are often all that's needed. In other classrooms, clusters of four desks pushed together to form a table create individual places for each student, but also a larger table for small-group work. In smaller classrooms, islands of eight desks (two rows of four desks facing each other) allow students to work with someone sitting across from them and also next to them. With any of these arrangements, students can easily work in pairs or fours, and can even come together as groups of eight to discuss their work. Some teachers have enough space in their classrooms for a separate meeting area where students gather for whole-class discussions; other teachers find that conducting whole-class discussions with students seated in their clusters works just as well and requires less time for transitions.

The visual impact of the classroom is also important. Think about it—when you walk into a room or an office, the first pieces of information you get about the environment are visual. Similarly, what is displayed on bulletin boards and on the walls of classrooms can tell you a great deal.

Imagine walking into a classroom: You see displays of three-dimensional toys that students have constructed out of interlocking cubes, along with instruction booklets they have written for making these toys. You see a bookshelf labeled "Classroom Authors." You see bean plants, some a bit straggly, growing along the windowsill with a growth graph next to each one. You also see large pieces of chart paper hanging around the perimeter of the room with titles like "Strategies for Measuring," "Conjectures About Odd and Even Numbers," and "Patterns We Found on the 100 Charts." All of these are documentation of students' work. The walls and shelves of a classroom are like a museum: They offer a history of the students' work and thinking and a source of information for students, teachers, administrators, and parents. These displays convey to students that their work is interesting, valuable, and ongoing—that even though a project or unit is over, we still reflect on those experiences over time and in new ways.

Contrast this interactive classroom environment with one that's filled with commercially made bulletin boards and teacher-made displays. We might ask ourselves, before putting something up on the walls of our classrooms, "What does this tell me about my students? What does this tell me about the learning experiences that go on in this room?"

Putting up ready-made pictures and displays, especially at the beginning of the year, may make the room seem friendlier and more welcoming. But there's another way to think about it: Suppose the students enter a classroom with empty walls and are told, "This is *your* classroom. During the next few weeks we will be creating an environment that is yours; soon your work will fill these empty walls." When students are part of establishing the classroom environment, they immediately feel more ownership of what they are doing.

If you are trying to make the change, thinking about the physical space of your classroom and how it can work for you and your students is an important aspect of "How to Begin." Be prepared to alter your plans once you have seen students working. While you don't want to change plans too often, a certain amount of flexibility is important as you figure out how the physical environment works best.

Storing the Tools for Learning

Constructivist curricula require that tools and manipulatives be available to students at all times. Students at all levels need to be able to use whatever tools they choose to solve problems, and they should make their own decisions about which material might best help them solve a problem. For example, for solving a mapping problem, they may want to use string or counters to measure, grid paper for drawing, and a calculator for adding up distances. Different strategies and methods of keeping track necessitate different materials.

Some teachers store their materials in a central "math center," which might be a separate bookshelf, a designated shelf in a closet, or containers of materials arranged along a windowsill. Other teachers arrange smaller centers around the classroom where students will be working on a variety of activity choices during math time. Common materials such as paper and calculators might be stored in a central place, but materials specific to each activity would be found in a designated "center," along with directions for the activity.

Once students are familiar with how and where materials are stored in their classroom, they should be expected to take responsibility not only for the daily cleanup, but also for checking that the math shelves are well organized and that items such as paper and pencils are restocked at the end of each week. Some teachers ask for volunteers to manage this task; others assign rotating pairs of students to this classroom job. Even teachers of younger grades find that if routines are well established and materials are clearly organized, students can take responsibility for their management.

"Having materials readily available" should convey to students the *expectation* that they will use these materials to solve problems. Traditionally, concrete objects like blocks and counters and even fingers were considered babyish; although sometimes used to introduce a new concept, they were quickly dismissed in favor of pencil and paper. Even worse, those students who needed extra help were often stigmatized by "*having* to use materials" because they "didn't get it" as quickly as others. In the traditional mathematics classroom, even the youngest student quickly gets the message that the goal of doing math is to use symbols and do it on paper. In a constructivist classroom, all students—as well as the teacher—use tools, drawings, and materials to solve problems. Manipulatives offer more ways for a range of students to enter and persist at difficult problems, a way of keeping track of work, and a way of representing solutions to problems.

Creating a Mathematical Community

How the physical space is organized and how students use materials to solve problems are certainly important, but perhaps the most vital component of a classroom community is how students interact with each other and how they "live" in the physical space. An important part of the teacher's job is to establish a classroom culture that encourages and promotes risk taking and that values and respects students' ideas. In such an environment, students are given significant responsibility in making choices—about how they will solve problems, what materials they will use, how they will keep track of their thinking and their work. The following questions can help teachers think about ways to create a challenging yet supportive classroom community:

- How can I ensure that thinking and reasoning will be at the center of each student's mathematical experience?

- How can I ensure that every student in this classroom is recognized for his or her contributions?

- How can I encourage risk taking?

- How can I support the mathematical learning of my students?

- How can I help my students create an environment that is a safe place for each and every one of us?

The answer to the last question is a good place to begin. Many teachers have found that having *one rule* in their classroom, about *being safe,* sets a tone for everything else that happens.

- Are students' ideas safe? Are they respected and listened to and considered as valuable information? Can anyone ask questions freely and without embarrassment?

- Is students' work safe? Is it taken care of, respected, and seen not just as "right" or "wrong" but as an expression of their thinking? Is it regarded as useful information to others?

- Are materials kept safe—used responsibly and taken care of?

- Are the students physically safe? Can they work without interruption and threat?

The physical environment and the curriculum contribute in many ways to establishing a safe classroom environment. Simply by working together, taking charge of tools and materials, making choices, and developing strategies that make sense instead of following rote procedures, students are starting to take responsibility for their own learning.

Setting the stage and setting the tone for the learning that will take place in the classroom is a big responsibility. However, not everything needs to happen at once. The community of active, engaged learners will unfold over time as long as we continue to hold high expectations for the students and encourage them to construct mathematics for themselves.

CHAPTER 4

Questions Teachers Ask

So, You're Skeptical

When reading and hearing about constructivist curricula, many teachers are concerned about whether this is the "new math" all over again. Will students who learn this way really understand the arithmetic that they need in order to solve commonplace problems? Or will they learn a lot of esoteric mathematics and come up short on basic skills? As a teacher said to one of our workshop leaders: "They [the new curricula] all sound the same. Kids work cooperatively, solve interesting problems, and don't do much computation."

Most teachers understand that the new curricula, as opposed to more traditional curricula, emphasize critical thinking skills, a broader range of mathematical content, group work, and affective factors. But at what cost? Are students who learn through these new curricula going to emerge as confident, cooperative, and critical thinkers who can't add?

These are fair questions, and this chapter provides direct answers to them. Before addressing these questions, we want everyone to be clear about one thing: It is true that children who invent their own methods for solving problems will not memorize the "standard" procedures for carrying, borrowing, multiplying, or dividing. *But they will definitely learn to add, subtract, multiply, and divide.* When they see traditional problems, like $354 - 198$ or $182 \div 16$, they will not only feel comfortable tackling these problems, they will have a wide range of options available for solving them. How will they do this if they can't carry, borrow, or use standard algorithms for multiplication and division? They will learn by taking charge of problem solving and constructing mathematics for themselves.

Giving up the "old" way of teaching has many implications, and it isn't easy. Teachers have many questions about turning away from the traditional and presumably valuable ways of teaching mathematics. In this chapter, we raise and address the questions we have heard most often. Even after reading these responses, you may remain skeptical. The best way to address this skepticism is to observe how this way of learning mathematics works in action. Find a teacher who is trying out some of these ideas—or better yet, try some of them yourself.

☞ **How exactly is the constructivist approach different?**

To illuminate the differences in the approaches, let's compare the traditional way of doing a basic word problem with a constructivist way. Consider the following problem for third graders, one that could conceivably appear in either a textbook or a newer math curriculum:

> *Martin Luther King was born in 1929 and was assassinated in 1968. How old would he be if he were alive today?*

Traditional Approach

Conceptualizing the problem.   This is a very difficult problem for students in a traditional math program. First, all the numerical information (e.g., this year's date) isn't given in the problem, and some extra information (e.g., the year 1968) is given. Students must figure out which information is relevant and that they need to make use of the current date to complete this problem. In addition, students steeped in a traditional approach would be expected to conceptualize this problem as a subtraction one. This is a huge intellectual leap for a third grader; finding out how old someone would be just does not feel like subtraction.

In fact, many third or fourth graders who have received traditional instruction would be unable to conceptualize this problem and would simply give up. They might say to the teacher, "Just tell me whether to divide, multiply, subtract, or add. Then I can solve it." In other words, they are asking someone else to conceptualize the problem for them.

Representing the problem.   With a traditional approach, there is one "right" way of representing this problem. It is:

$$1996 \text{ (or current year)}$$
$$-\underline{1929}$$

Note that the problem is written vertically. Students in traditional programs are taught that this is the correct way to set up a problem for subtraction. There is no encouragement to represent the problem in a different way, such as by using addition, or by setting up a time line (very useful in this instance), or by using any other kind of representation.

Solving the problem. For students in traditional programs, this is the straightforward part. They have been taught a procedure for borrowing, and they would apply it to this problem and get an answer in the following way:

$$
\begin{array}{r}
{\scriptstyle 8\ 16} \\
19\cancel{9}\cancel{6} \\
-\underline{1929} \\
67
\end{array}
$$

Interpreting the problem and its solution.   The discussion of this problem would probably not take long. With one strategy for doing it, the only differences in students' approaches might be that some of them borrowed incorrectly.

Constructivist Approach

Conceptualizing the problem.   Students in constructivist classrooms would be accustomed to thinking about problems like these. They would feel no pressure to think about this problem as subtraction, addition, or any other operation. In all likelihood, they'd think about this problem as "How far is it from one number to another?" or "How many years is it from 1929 to 1996?" Some might think about it in two steps: "How long did Martin Luther King live, or how far is it from 1929 to 1968?" and "How many years has it been since Martin Luther King died?" They would then consider combining these two numbers to answer the question. Students in constructivist curricula are familiar with more complicated problems like this, and they have experience selecting and using relevant information.

Representing the problem. In a constructivist curriculum, students would understand that there are *many* ways to represent this problem. They would be familiar with the standard representations of this problem and would also invent their own to solve it. In addition to the subtraction problem, which is the conventional representation, they would know that this problem can be represented by addition: 1929 + _____ = 1996. We would expect students to know that addition and subtraction are both good ways of describing the same problem.

This kind of problem would also generate many invented representations in a constructivist classroom. Some students with less sophisticated strategies for solving addition and subtraction problems might begin by representing the problem as shown in Example A.

Example A

1929 — 0 years old (just born)

1930 — 1 year old

1931 — 2 years old

1932 — 3 years old

(and so forth)

Sometimes, students continue to solve a problem like this by representing consecutive "jumps" from one number to the next. At some point, they often see that they can take bigger jumps (Example B).

Example B

1929 — 0

1930 — 1 year old

1940 — 11 (1 year + 10 years)

1950 — 21

(and so forth)

Some children might represent this data on a horizontal number line, and show the jumps from year to year or from decade to decade (Example C).

Example C

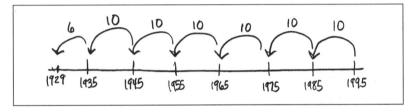

Whatever method they choose or invent to represent the problem, students in a constructivist curriculum would know that it is their responsibility to keep track of how they are solving the problem by recording their "moves." Students quickly get the idea that the more complicated the problem, the more important it is to keep track of beginning, intermediate, and final steps in solving it. The student who used the time line (Example C) wrote down all the decades to keep track. While some might be able to do all this counting without keeping track, an important mathematical task is to learn *when* and *how* to keep track in order to make the thinking process easier.

Solving the problem.   In a constructivist classroom, representing and solving the problem go hand in hand. Usually, a student's representation tells you something about how he or she chooses to solve the problem. The students who write down every year in a sequence (Example A) are solving the problem by counting on by ones. This is a tedious method, but one that they can be sure of. By working with peers and seeing their strategies, as well as by becoming more comfortable with how the number system works, students who start out relying on ones will eventually start making bigger jumps. Soon they will become comfortable with using tens as they come to see how this works and that it is more efficient. In the meantime, they are able to engage, on their own level, with a problem that would traditionally be considered beyond their reach. The second student (Example B) is making bigger jumps, adding on in order to solve the problem while making good use of decades or "landmarks" in the number system. The third student (Example C) jumps backward in order to solve the problem. This third approach makes good use of a number line to show what happens as we subtract tens.

These are not the only methods of solving the problem, of course. Some students develop more complex strategies that solve the problem with very few intermediate steps. Here's a strategy from a student who began with the standard vertical format:

$$
\begin{array}{r}
1996 \\
-\underline{1929} \\
-3 \\
70 \\
70 - 3 = 67
\end{array}
$$

This child never learned to borrow. Her approach was to subtract 9 from 6, and correctly arrive at –3. Then she subtracted 20 from 90 and arrived at 70. She combined these two figures, getting the correct result. (Try out this method with other numbers; it always works.) She used what she knew about "counting below zero" in order to do the subtraction. In order to check her solution, she counted on in decades from 1929, saying quietly to herself "1939 is 10, 1949 is 20 . . . 1989 is 60, and from 1989 to 1996 is 7 more, so 67."

Interpreting the problem and its solution.   Students who are used to thinking mathematically are likely to delve into this problem on a far deeper level than their peers in traditional classrooms. In fact, with problems like these, teachers are accustomed to hearing children grapple with complete birth dates—*month* and *day,* in addition to *year.* They report good mathematical discussions over such issues as whether Martin Luther King would be 67 at the very beginning of 1996, or if he would have to wait until his birthday in order to reach 67.

Some teachers worry that the plethora of problem-solving strategies that can arise when students invent their own approaches will be confusing to students. Why not introduce the straightforward, standard way of doing a problem like the one about Martin Luther King and teach everyone this method? The problem is that the "standard" way of doing the task neither connects to nor arises from children's developing understanding of the number system. Because it doesn't connect to their own understanding, many students will be confused by the standard way, no matter how many times you teach it. And even students who "get" the standard way of doing it have not necessarily made sense of it. They may just be parroting it back and will probably get confused when they try to apply the algorithm to an unfamiliar problem. By teaching the standard method, we are getting in the way of mathematical thinking rather than promoting it. Only by solving problems themselves, and by figuring out whether their answers make sense, will children build a deep understanding of what numbers mean.

☞ Shouldn't students memorize the basic math facts?

Even if we encourage students to use their own strategies to puzzle through arithmetic problems, isn't it important for them to memorize the basic facts and be able to recall them quickly and accurately? This is a multifaceted question.

Yes, elementary school students should become very familiar with the basic addition, subtraction, multiplication, and division facts. But math educators are finding it essential that students' familiarity grow out of lots of experience with constructing these facts on their own (Gray and Tall, 1994). Just as we become familiar with a dance step by doing it many times, on different occasions, with different music, students become familiar with basic operations by using them often in different contexts. After a while, they will be able to remember many or most of the more simple calculations. Keep in mind that some students remember more easily than others, and that lack of a good memory should not interfere with being a good mathematician.

Memorization isn't the goal; *fluency* is. Yes, students should be able to give the answer to 9×8. But many children and adults—even those of us who have drilled our way through several years of math class—do forget on occasion. The important thing is that students be able to use their knowledge of numbers to fluently reconstruct calculations that may be difficult for them to remember. If you don't remember 9×8, you can easily derive it by using your knowledge of 10×8, then subtracting the extra 8. A fluent math user will apply strategies like this often, and in the process will be learning a great deal about mathematical relationships. Teachers need to encourage rather than discourage these strategies.

Speed is not the goal; *fluency* is. Yes, students need to be able to recall $9 + 5$ relatively quickly. But does it really make any difference whether a second grader can do this in 5 seconds or 1 second? Given 5 seconds, a child who doesn't remember this fact could be thinking, "$10 + 5$ is 15, so $9 + 5$ is 1 less, or 14." When students feel time pressure, these excellent strategies for reconstructing math facts tend to fly out the window. That is why we do not recommend the use of timed math tests, especially those that time students on how quickly they can recall math facts. The speedy recollection of facts shouldn't be confused with real mathematical skill. Good mathematical strategies—not quick memorization—are what really matters in understanding mathematics. Thinking may sometimes slow students down, but in slowing down, they get essential practice in constructing number relationships. It's important not to sacrifice understanding in the pursuit of efficiency.

Here's another important thing to remember about arithmetic: Only a very small part of it is these memorized "facts." Teachers and curriculum writers sometimes forget that students need to become fluent with all aspects of the number system, not just with basic operations. We should expect much more of students than the simple memorization of a small collection of "facts"; we should expect them to use their knowledge of the number system to construct an unlimited number of combinations, differences, products, and "fair shares," and to do it fluently.

☞ **Don't students need to learn the fundamental math algorithms?**

Everyone needs to know a couple of good ways to add, subtract, multiply, and divide. However, the ways that we were taught to do these operations aren't necessarily the best or most efficient ways. Believe it or not, these traditional algorithms are largely the result of historical accident. Borrowing, carrying, the procedure for long division—they're not universal. In other countries and at other times in our own country, students have been taught different and equally effective algorithms for the basic operations. Constructing effective algorithms, ones that can be used efficiently in a range of different situations, is in itself an important element of mathematical thinking. Students who invent algorithms that are easy to use are doing significant mathematical work. On the other hand, applying someone else's algorithms to solve a problem—especially if you have no understanding of how or why these algorithms work—is not "doing mathematics."

Many of us still believe that the four operations are one and the same as the algorithms we were taught in school, and that today's students must learn these procedures in order to "master" arithmetic. Certainly long division is something we equate with the algorithm. Faced with a problem like $375 \div 25$, we are likely to write out the long division procedure—figure out how many times 25 will fit into 37, do the multiplication, then the subtraction ($37 - 25 = 12$), then bring down the final 5. But does this procedure make sense in this context? It is neither the most elegant, the easiest, nor the most efficient way of doing the problem. In the time it took you to write the problem down, you could easily have said, "I know there are four 25's in 100, so there are sixteen 25's in 400. There's one less in 375, so it's 15." Furthermore, the algorithm for long division is one that very few adults can explain (Simon, 1993). How then can elementary students hope to explain how the long division algorithm works?

It's easy to think of many situations in which the standard American algorithm is an *inefficient* way of doing an operation. Adding 1987 + 1013 is another good example. Here's the standard algorithm:

$$
\begin{array}{r}
{\scriptstyle 1\ 1} \\
1987 \\
+\underline{1013} \\
3000
\end{array}
$$

The algorithm involves three rounds of carrying—an inefficient procedure under the circumstances. We should know enough about number relations to look at the 13 + 87 and immediately conclude that it's 100, or to look at the 987 + 13 and conclude that it's 1000. The standard approach to doing this problem is cumbersome; it breaks the problem into little pieces, when the most efficient way of solving it is to work with the big picture.

In the *Investigations* curriculum, standard algorithms are not taught because they interfere with a child's growing number sense and fluency with the number system. Of course, students are encouraged to invent their own good algorithms and to share these with their peers. If they already know standard algorithms, they are asked to explain how these work. By seeing each other's strategies, students will encounter a wide range of approaches for doing arithmetic. Ultimately, their repertoire of arithmetic skills will be much wider than if they simply learned the traditional algorithms. They will be able to match their strategy with the demands of the particular problem they encounter. In the end, students who use what they know about number relations to do arithmetic are the most effective and flexible problem solvers.

Some teachers ask, how about teaching new algorithms to replace the old ones? For example, when students use their own strategies, they are likely to add from left to right, starting with higher numbers and then moving on to lower ones. In a problem like the one above (1987 + 1013), they would start with the thousands, move on to hundreds, then combine the tens and ones. This is, of course, backwards from the traditional algorithmic method of adding. Recent research has shown that left-to-right strategies make much more sense to students, are less confusing to them, and promote learning (Kamii and Lewis, 1993). Why not just teach this approach? The answer is this: Even this very good strategy for adding doesn't work for all students on all problems. The point isn't to find better algorithms to replace the old ones; rather, it is to identify and encourage the students' own good strategies for making sense of the operations.

Many of the newer math curricula attempt to teach traditional algorithms through manipulatives like base-ten blocks, rods, and cubes. Students are expected to use manipulatives to carry out a particular procedure, usually one that is based on the algorithm. For example, students might model an addition problem like 46 + 15 with tens and ones blocks, and trade units for tens whenever they reach a number of 10 or more. While this is a more concrete way of teaching the traditional algorithm, that algorithm may get in the way of real mathematical thinking. Whenever students use a standard algorithm, they need to be able to explain—or show with manipulatives—how it works. This same expectation holds true for any strategy that a student uses.

☞ **Isn't it inefficient to reinvent the wheel each time you solve a problem?**

This question has a two-part answer. First, it's important that for the first few times students encounter a new type of problem, they figure out their own strategies for addressing it. Someone else may have invented another way, but it will not be as useful to students as the ways they discover on their own. Yes, the process may be inefficient—but only at first.

Then, once students have developed a couple of good strategies and have seen the strategies that others use, we wouldn't expect them to reinvent the wheel whenever they encounter similar problems. With the teacher's encouragement, they will gravitate toward one or two strategies that work best for them, then use these in many different situations. They will also see that different strategies are efficient in different situations. Multiplying by 9 may well involve a different strategy than multiplying by 4. Multiplying 1346 × 231 is a problem that is best solved with a calculator, while 500 × 200 is easily done with mental arithmetic (assuming a good knowledge of the structure of the number system). Problems are different, and good mathematicians adapt their strategies to suit the problem.

Students need practice in using their strategies if they are to become efficient at using them. By practice, we do not mean repetitive drill or page after page of similar problems. Rather, students need many experiences with related kinds of problems. Efficiency isn't abandoned in a constructivist curriculum; it's simply something that comes over time, after the students have constructed their own problem-solving methods and understand why they work.

☞ If we're not teaching algorithms, do we give up standard notation, too?

Teachers often ask what they are to do about standard notation for arithmetic if they are not teaching the algorithms. Is notation—the plus (+) and minus (–) signs, times (× or •) and division (÷ or / or ⌐) signs—something that we should expect children to learn? Yes! The symbols used to denote multiplication, addition, subtraction, and division are the universal way of communicating about these operations. The symbols for the operations are important because they communicate *what* arithmetic is being done. Just remember, though, that these symbols are not a recipe telling us *how* to do the arithmetic.

Students need to recognize what these symbols mean and how to use them in as many different contexts as possible. Furthermore, they need to learn that symbols can be used in either horizontal or vertical formats. Researchers have discovered that many students are accustomed to seeing only one format (usually a vertical one) for certain kinds of problems, and have real trouble using the same symbols when problems are presented horizontally (Kamii, Lewis, and Livingston, 1993).

As students learn what the symbols communicate, they need to learn certain conventions—for example, that we can use numbers with a plus sign interchangeably (8 + 2 or 2 + 8) and get the same results, and that the same flexibility applies to multiplication (8 × 2 = 2 × 8). However, through their own experiences in communicating and miscommunicating the results of subtraction and division, students will learn that the order of numbers is important in some contexts; 8 – 2 is *not* the same as 2 – 8. No one needs to tell students that 2 – 8 is wrong, or that "you can't take 8 away from 2" (because, in fact, you can.) But students will find out that the results are different when the order changes. They will learn that the grammar of arithmetic, like the grammar of written language, makes an enormous difference: It allows you to say exactly what you mean.

☞ **Doesn't using the calculator interfere with students' learning of arithmetic?**

Traditionally, the major goal of mathematics education was to train students in the use of reliable, efficient, and speedy procedures for adding, subtracting, multiplying, and dividing. You can still see this goal reflected in many mathematics curricula. It was argued that students needed this emphasis on calculation and "accounting math" in order to prepare them for jobs and for the everyday business of running a household.

It is just as true today that students need to be able to solve job- and household-related problems involving the basic arithmetic operations. Above all, they need to be able to decide how and when to use these operations to solve a variety of problems (none of which will announce themselves as ready-made, worksheet-like computation problems). But today's students have an important tool available to them: the calculator. With a calculator, students can focus on the important parts of mathematical problem solving: figuring out what the problem is asking, representing it in a way that makes sense, using good number sense to estimate the answer, and interpreting the answer. The procedure itself is the most routine aspect of the problem, one well suited to a nonintelligent $5 machine.

Steven Leinwand, in his article "It's Time to Abandon Computational Algorithms" (1994), eloquently describes the changes that calculators should be bringing to our mathematics classrooms:

A few short years ago we had few or no alternatives to pencil-and-paper computation. A few short years ago we could even justify the pain and frustration we witnessed in our classes as necessary parts of learning what were then important skills. Today there are alternatives and there is no honest way to justify the psychic toll it takes. We need to admit that drill and practice of computational algorithms devour an incredibly large proportion of instructional time, precluding any real chance for actually applying mathematics and developing the conceptual understanding that underlies mathematical literacy. (p. 36)

What is the implication for math teaching? There is no longer a justifiable reason for asking students to do pages of calculations—especially more time-consuming calculations like adding series of numbers or multiplying three-digit numbers by other three-digit numbers. We do not want to waste students' time on frustrating tasks that involve the rote application of memorized algorithms. Before asking your students to do problems *without* a calculator, ask yourself how you'd do the problem yourself. Would you grab a calculator if it were handy? If so, let your students do the same! You would probably not use a calculator to figure out 35 × 11, 21 – 19, or even $10.94 + $1.07. You easily use mental arithmetic to come up with quick and accurate answers. We want students to be able to do this, too. But calculators should be available nearly all the time, so that students can do more difficult calculations or check the answers that they arrived at using their own strategies.

Teachers often ask whether calculators will prevent children from learning arithmetic. In well over 100 research studies, mathematics test scores have shown that children who use calculators do as well as or better than those who do not use them (Hembree and Dessart, 1986; Suydam, 1986). Calculators give children more time to focus on the truly important aspects of numerical reasoning.

☛ **Can't I combine the traditional way of teaching with a constructivist way of teaching math—to get the best of both worlds?**

Some teachers who begin using a constructivist curricula try to hedge their bets by teaching *both* a constructivist approach to operations like multiplication *and* the traditional procedures. Is there anything wrong with this? Yes, here's what's wrong: In classrooms where both approaches are used to teach a skill, children become confused about when they are supposed to use their own strategies for figuring out a problem and when they are supposed to use the officially sanctioned approach. Children get the sense that:

- Their own approach to problem-solving is merely "exploration," and they will later learn the "right" way.

- Their own approach isn't as good as the one the teacher shows.

- The teacher didn't really mean it when he or she said there were lots of good strategies for solving problems like 34×68.

You can probably see the conflict. It's like telling your children they can make their own decision about something, then telling them what their decision ought to be. As you know, children see through these contradictions very quickly.

There is growing evidence that "Algorithms unteach place value and prevent children from developing number sense" (Kamii, Lewis, and Livingston, 1993, p. 202). Students who are developing their own strategies are in some ways quite vulnerable. If you pull the rug out from under them by substituting a "better" way, they will learn that their own ways are inferior. If you truly believe that the traditional way is better, it may be best to stick with what you know rather than giving your students mixed messages.

Teachers often have important *practical* reasons for using both kinds of curricula simultaneously: The parents want to see more worksheets; an achievement test focusing on computation is coming up; the teacher in the next grade insists that kids know the procedure for long division. We talk more about how to handle these issues in chapter 5, but the fact is, students who use a constructivist curriculum and do not learn any standard computational procedures perform *just as well* on untimed computation as their peers. Furthermore, research studies from this country and from international comparisons have shown that students who use their own procedures do quite a bit better than students who use standard ones (Stevenson, Lee, and Stigler, 1986; Fennema, Carpenter, and Peterson, 1989). They may be slower in computational speed, but they won't fall behind in understanding. A more legitimate worry is that students will learn and understand so much math that they will be bored if and when they go back to a traditional approach to arithmetic. But that's not a bad worry to have.

☞ Why can't we teach the basics first, then let the kids experiment with their own strategies?

This question is related to the preceding one about simultaneously using traditional and constructivist approaches. Some teachers believe that it's all right for students to use their own strategies as an alternative for figuring out problems only *after* they have learned "the basics." The problem with this sequential strategy relates to the perceived need for invented strategies: Why develop your own strategy if you've already been shown the "right" way? It's almost as if the teacher is saying, "If you can't do it the right way, then go ahead and use your own way." The belief that students should be free to experiment only after they know the proper technique is different from constructivism, which asserts that the best way to learn the basics of mathematics is by doing it for yourself.

☞ What will happen to my students next year, if they go back to a more traditional mathematics curriculum?

Many teachers who are trying the constructivist approach wonder whether their students, now learning about constructing mathematics for themselves, will be at a disadvantage when and if they return to a more traditional mathematics curriculum. Unless an entire school or district is committed to making the shift, it may be a reasonable assumption that students will soon find themselves in a traditional curriculum—if not next year, then perhaps the following year.

While this is unfortunate, no teachers need worry that their students will be at a long-term disadvantage. Common sense suggests that students who have learned to do mathematics on their own, to decide which strategies work and how they work, and to figure out different ways of solving mathematical problems will in fact have a certain advantage. These students will want to make sense out of mathematics, and they will know from experience that it is possible to do so. If the mathematical procedures being taught don't make sense to them, they will have many tools for working out their own ways that do make sense. These students will not be so likely to panic if they don't know the right answer or the right operation. They will be well prepared for the variety of mathematics they encounter in the future because they will be used to actually *doing* mathematics.

As we discuss in chapter 6, there are many ways of making constructivist mathematics an ongoing and more visible part of the entire school community. While you may not be able to change the teaching approach of next year's classroom teacher, there is still much that you can do to build a school climate that values mathematical problem solving. If students from this year's class routinely encounter interactive "problems of the week" in the hallway, or if you ask some of them back to present their work during a schoolwide math night for parents, they will be reminded of the beauty and power of meaningful mathematics. If higher grade classes can be involved in some of your data-gathering activities (for example, are fifth graders different from fourth graders in the amount of sleep that they get?), this involvement can help maintain past students' interest in the mathematical thinking that they did when they were in your classroom.

☞ **Is it an important part of constructivist learning that the problems have "real" contexts?**

Many constructivist curricula emphasize mathematical problems that have a "real-life" or applied context. Like adults, children are drawn to problems that offer an inherent reason for solving them. Figuring out how much of each ingredient to buy for a class cooking project, how many school supplies the class will use up in a year, or how the chairs and tables can fit better in the classroom—all of these are good examples of applied problems. At the same time, many other types of mathematical problems are both important and motivating, yet have no worldly context. Determining how many 1-inch cubes will fit in an irregular solid is a compelling geometric problem for fifth graders, despite the apparent lack of applications in the real world. Similarly, determining the relationship between the triangle-shaped pattern block and the hexagonal one is mathematically intriguing for many primary grade students, even though they aren't concerned about how to tile their bathrooms. Problems like these draw students in because the mathematics itself is intriguing. Students are easily attracted to the aesthetics of a tessellation, and often enjoy the puzzle-like challenge of figuring out a mathematical pattern.

Seven-year-old Jacob recently began a mathematical quest to find all possible ways to subtract one number from another to make 24. He chose this problem on his own. He started with 25 – 1, 26 – 2, 27 – 3, and continued with this pattern for some time. The fact that he would still get 24, even as the numbers got bigger and bigger, fascinated him. After half an hour, he had three pages of systematic calculations to proudly show to his parents and, later, to his class. He continued with this problem for several more days, at which point he confidently announced to his mother, "I think there's a thousand ways to make 24, and I'm going to find them all." Discovering the mathematical possibilities is an exciting proposition for children, a proposition that need not be limited to the mundane realities of the world. The beauty of mathematics is that it allows us to solve everyday problems, to play with everyday and fantasy situations, and quite often, to transcend our everyday reality.

CHAPTER 5

A New Kind of Assessment

Old Tests, New Skills

When introducing a new mathematics curriculum into the classroom, a key problem is that there aren't ready-made ways of finding out exactly what students are learning. Moreover, there are no easy ways of examining *how* students' mathematical thinking is developing. Most traditional curricula go hand in hand with just about any standardized mathematics achievement test that you can buy off the shelf. These tests are well matched to the old curriculum's emphasis on speed, computation, memorization, and formulas and definitions. But researchers, teachers, and administrators all agree that these old tests cannot measure deep mathematical understanding any better than a ruler can measure the national debt.

Traditional math curricula make it relatively easy to develop quizzes, checklists, and assignments to assess students' learning. Generating test problems by substituting different numbers into problems presented in the textbook, counting how many problems each student gets correct, and determining scores or grades based on this number—traditional assessment often seems that simple. The reform movement in mathematics asks much more of assessment: It asks that teachers truly examine students' mathematical work, question students about their thinking, and observe their strategies for solving challenging, multifaceted problems. This deeper probing of the progress in students' thinking lies at the heart of a constructivist approach. Assessment and teaching depend on the same critical ingredient: a solid understanding of students' mathematical thinking.

What Is the Purpose of Assessment?

Assessment should be the servant of teaching and learning. Without information about their students' skills, understanding, and individual approaches to mathematics, teachers have nothing to guide their work. They must fall back on someone else's prescription for what should be taught to first graders, and what the students "will master" during the school year. Rather than such prescriptions, teachers need to gather their own evidence about how students learn. By building student assessment into their teaching as much as possible, teachers can use the information garnered from that assessment to guide their classroom practice.

Teachers who become attuned to examining students' mathematical conversations, writing, products, and activities reap many benefits. Most important, they gain a thorough understanding of each child's strengths and weaknesses. Rather than simply knowing that "Johnny hasn't mastered two-digit subtraction," a teacher who makes assessment an integral part of his or her practice will know, for example, that Johnny views subtraction problems only as "taking away," that he doesn't yet think about *comparison* as a form of subtraction, and that he takes away objects one by one and recalculates the total each time he does so. This teacher has a much firmer foundation for figuring out where to go next with Johnny and may, for example, decide he needs to play more games that involve jumping backwards on the 100 chart or number line, or to do more activities that involve comparing two amounts. Or, the teacher may decide to pair Johnny with a student who has recently progressed from counting back one at a time to counting back by tens. Johnny's teacher isn't obliged to do this detailed planning and decision making each day for each child, but the information collected through regular observation enables a teacher to make these decisions when time allows.

On a broader level, evidence about how *all* students in the class are learning helps a teacher decide more generally about where and how to proceed with the math curriculum. For example, are many students confused about how to determine the number of objects in two-dimensional arrays? If so, the students may need additional work—perhaps reinforced with home activities—in finding and examining different arrays in their immediate world. On the other hand, if many students are eagerly and accurately constructing two-dimensional arrays, it may be time to challenge them with constructing jumbo-sized arrays, or arrays with many layers (three-dimensional arrays). If the students in the class are at very different levels in their understanding of arrays, it's probably time to think about which members of each group need (or can provide) more help, and how to stretch the curriculum's activities in different directions to meet the needs of the different students.

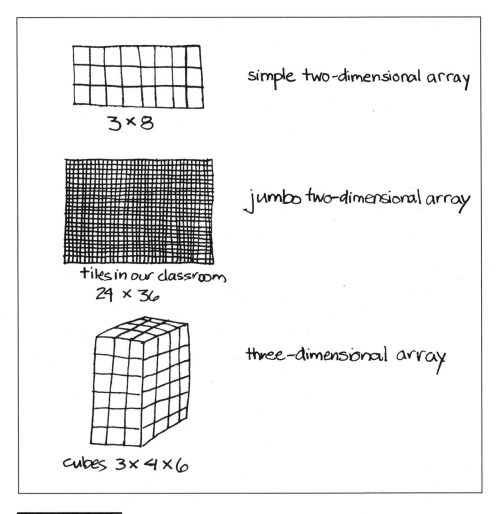

simple two-dimensional array

3 × 8

jumbo two-dimensional array

tiles in our classroom
24 × 36

three-dimensional array

cubes 3 × 4 × 6

Arrays are one way to help students visualize multiplication relationships. Within a single class, some students may need more work with simple two-dimensional arrays while others are ready for jumbo-sized or even three-dimensional arrays. Your assessment can help you adjust the curriculum to meet these individual needs.

The purpose of assessment should also be to help students learn. In a good curriculum, assessments do not take time away from learning, but instead contribute to learning. From the student's perspective, assessment should be indistinguishable from any other good mathematical activity. Assessment activities can involve drawing, representing, discussing, making things, and writing. They might be done individually, with partners, in small groups, or by the class as a whole. Sometimes, assessment activities encourage students to be more explicit than usual in their talking or writing about solutions to a problem. For example, students may be asked to write an explanation of their favorite strategies for solving a problem or playing a game. Assessment activities should encourage communication about mathematical ideas. As a side benefit, students will often begin to see for themselves what they do and do not understand. This self-awareness is an integral part of learning.

Here is what assessment in a constructivist curriculum is *not* about: It is not about ranking students, determining ability groupings, or figuring out who is ready for acceleration. In the *Investigations* curriculum, for example, you will find no timed tests, no assessments that rank students, and no specific guidance about how the suggested assessment can be translated into grades. There are three reasons for this approach: first, because we believe that the "ranking" aspects of assessment have received entirely too much attention in the past, causing the more important purposes of assessment to be lost; second, because we believe that assessment for the sake of labeling students or comparing them with others can be damaging; and third, because mathematical understanding is complex and multidimensional, and cannot be meaningfully reduced to a single grade, percentile, or set of scores.

Of course, the reality in many schools is that teachers need to assign numerical scores and grades. We know this will happen. However, teachers themselves are in the best position to understand their particular school's policies about grading and to make decisions about how to translate assessment information into grades. Teachers who are required to grade don't need complicated scoring frameworks. They *do* need a clear sense of their own priorities and their mathematical goals for students.

Transforming open-ended assessment into grades is dependent on a teacher's values. How much should effort count? How much do we look at development over the whole semester as opposed to an absolute level of performance? How do we weigh *proficiency* versus *fluency* versus *flexibility of thinking?* These philosophical questions are beyond the scope of this book, but they are addressed thoughtfully in several new books on alternative assessment (NCTM, 1995; Hart, 1994; Mitchell, 1992; Perrone, 1991). A particularly interesting discussion of "the grading dilemma" is presented in Lew Romangnano's (1994) book about his firsthand difficulties and successes in teaching mathematics from a constructivist perspective.

Assessment is collecting evidence for a purpose that extends beyond grading. If we don't plan to use that evidence to guide what the class will do next, or to figure out why Luisa is having problems with fractions (and to help her overcome her problems), or to piece together how Ty's understanding of geometry helps him solve problems involving number, then there really is no point to collecting the evidence in the first place. Whatever assessments we choose to do or construct, they should be useful to our teaching. Equally important, assessments should be a meaningful learning experience for the students. Assessments take valuable class time for teachers and students alike—let's make that time meaningful.

How to Make Assessment Part of Teaching

How do you begin to do the kind of assessment that plays such a critical role in teaching and learning? This is relatively uncharted territory, and even the assessment experts do not agree on how to capture the essence of students' mathematical understanding. The alternatives they have generated—including portfolio assessment, clinical interviews, and open-ended items accompanied by elaborate scoring rubrics—provide an overwhelming amount of evidence of student learning, but are often complex, time-consuming, and difficult to interpret. Sorting through this evidence and forming a picture of how each student does mathematics threatens to be so labor-intensive that a teacher has no time left to teach.

Many new curricula make the assessment process a little easier by providing "embedded" assessments right in the curriculum. Some of these are simply questions to ask students in order to find out how they are thinking, or questions to ask yourself as you walk around the classroom observing students. Other embedded assessments involve collecting and analyzing student work on longer-term projects. These are all tools that a teacher can use to learn more about students' thinking. While teachers will each want to collect evidence in their own preferred way, assessments that are built into the curriculum provide some starting points and ideas. Whatever assessments you use, being curious about how your students think and learn is the main ingredient you'll need to effectively assess their thinking on an ongoing basis.

Checking In

As chapter 3 demonstrates, the role of the teacher is quite different in classrooms where students are actively engaged in mathematics. When students are busy working on projects, consulting team members, playing mathematical games with partners, and making choices about which activities they want to do next, *teachers* have the opportunity to observe students' work and to "talk mathematics" with them (Corwin, et al., 1995). In other words, teachers can use these work periods to check in with their students and gather information about what and how they are learning. Remember that by observing and asking good questions, we are also promoting learning. At first, it may be hard to figure out exactly how to do this "checking in." A teacher may be unsure about what to look for while moving from group to group, or may not know what kinds of questions to ask the students while observing them at work. The focus will, of course, depend on the mathematics that the students are doing, but we can ask ourselves some general questions to guide our observations and conversations with students, as the following examples demonstrate.

☞ **Do students come up with their own strategies for solving problems, or do they expect me to tell them exactly what to do? What do their strategies tell me about their mathematical understanding?**

Example: Students are playing Close to 100, a card game with the goal of making with number cards two 2-digit numbers that total as close as possible to 100—for example, 73 and 26. As you wander over to a group that is playing this game, two students almost grab you and demand to know which of their cards would make the best choices. You ask them what they think, and they look at you blankly. You point to a number made by two cards next to each other and ask them to figure out how large a number they would need to go with it. This question provides a focus, and the students get back to work.

In the meantime, another group member is carefully choosing two numbers from his cards. You ask him how he made his choices, and he explains, "I knew that 30 and 70 was exactly 100, but I didn't have two zeros, so I made 29 and 70, which is just 1 less."

You record on a note card that Alice and Marisa (the first two students) need more support in generating their own strategies, and that Roscoe (the third student) understands how to use multiples of 10 in reaching 100, as well as how to make adjustments in working with these multiples.

☞ **Do students understand that there are different strategies for solving problems? Do they articulate their strategies and listen to others' strategies?**

Example: There's an argument in one corner of the classroom and you go over to find out what's happening. The students are trying to find out how many more beans there are in one container (78) than another (56). Emma insists that you can find it by subtracting, and she has written out the problem and figured the correct answer. Karen states loudly that subtraction is wrong, because you're not taking away anything. She prefers to do the problem by counting on from 56 to 78, one at a time, and then shows just how she did this. You ask Emma how she got her answer. She says "by subtraction," and cannot elaborate when you ask her more about this. She does not seem to know why she chose subtraction. You ask the children to figure out why they came up with the same answer, and ask them to try their methods again with a slightly different problem.

You record that Emma seems stuck with a method of comparing that is correct, but she cannot explain her answer. Karen is able to explain how her quite basic strategy works. Neither girl seems to understand at this point that different strategies can work perfectly well for the same problem.

☞ **Do students have ideas about how to record their work, or does writing and drawing about what they have done seem difficult for them?**

Example: The students are working individually with data they have collected about the number and kinds of advertisements on TV. Eric is making a chart, recording the number of food commercials, car commercials, and toy commercials he observed. He's carefully checking the total, to see if he has counted correctly. He tells you, "I'm trying to come up with a way to show that I've got three times as many food commercials as toy commercials." You talk about what you see in his chart and what he wants it to show. He ends up thinking of a couple of possibilities for making the chart clearer.

You note that Eric is not only careful in checking his work and recording, but is also trying to develop new representations for showing the relationship between sizes more clearly. You also note that he has seen a relationship in his data that involves multiples and chooses to highlight this relationship.

☞ **Do students choose tools and materials that help them with their work? Do they use materials and tools effectively?**

Example: The students are working in small groups to figure out how many shoes there are in their classroom. Most of the students are using counters, cubes, or paper clips to count out the shoes by twos. In one group, Rosita is putting out pairs of cubes next to names on a class list. You ask her what the group is planning to do next. She explains that she will put down two cubes next to each child on the list, then simply count up all the cubes. Kirin, another student in the group, explains that they will count them by twos, and shows you how they will do this. The third child in the group, Samir, says that he's going to check their work on the calculator by adding 2 + 2 + 2 + 2 and so on, once they have all the cubes laid out.

You make a note that this group has a combination of strategies and tools that will enable them to solve the problem very well. They understand that the 2 + 2 + 2 ... operation on the calculator is similar to the laying out of two cubes for each student. Their use of the class list shows real strength in recording and keeping track.

Questions to Use for Ongoing Assessment

- Do students come up with their own strategies for solving problems, or do they expect me to tell them exactly what to do? What do their strategies tell me about their mathematical understanding?

- Do students understand that there are different strategies for solving problems? Do they articulate their strategies and listen to others' strategies?

- Do students choose tools and materials that help them with their work? Do they use these materials and tools effectively?

- Do students have ideas about how to record their work, or does writing and drawing about what they have done seem difficult for them?

Students will need time to become comfortable with the checking-in process, particularly if they are not accustomed to having teachers ask them about how they are thinking. One member of the *Investigations* assessment team recently worked with a fourth grader on a problem involving how many dogs could weigh the same as a baby elephant. After reviewing the weights and talking about how there were many different ways to solve the problem, the interviewer asked the student to explain or show how she was thinking about the problem. At that, the girl became quiet and withdrawn; she either could not or did not want to explain how she was thinking. However, after a few minutes, she announced the correct answer. When asked how she got there, she said nothing. This child clearly was unaccustomed to being asked about her thinking. It takes time for students to learn that we care more about their strategies than we do about getting a right answer. We need to be patient in order to reap the full benefits of checking in.

As we become more effective at checking in with students, and as they become more comfortable with us in this role, new ways of finding out how they are thinking are bound to emerge. Mainly, we need to keep our questions open-ended and to show genuine interest in how the students are approaching the task. If they sense that we are looking for a "right" way of doing the problem, students will keep searching for direct and nonverbal clues from us about what this right way is. When, however, they see that we are interested in their thinking and are counting on them to come up with their own ways of solving problems, they may well surprise us with the mathematics they can do.

Examining Students' Work

Checking in with students as they work is a staple form of ongoing assessment, but it doesn't always give us the opportunity to see how all students in the class are developing their mathematical understanding. It's just too hard to get a chance to observe and talk with everyone, even over the course of a week or longer. That's why we need to examine students' written work and constructions in order to find out more about their thinking. There is another benefit to this form of assessment: It gives students themselves a chance to examine, interpret, and explain their work in writing, and to understand how they are growing mathematically.

As students undertake investigations and projects, they should always be encouraged to document their work. They can keep notes, drawings, models, and rough drafts of their work as a project progresses—just as they would with writing assignments. For example, second grade students who are collecting data about "what scares second graders" will probably recategorize their data a few times before they come up with a scheme that really works. We can show them that we value this *process* of analysis by asking them to turn in drafts of their categories (along with all the relevant data) at different points in their work. Their final draft might be accompanied by a piece of writing about why they think their categories work well.

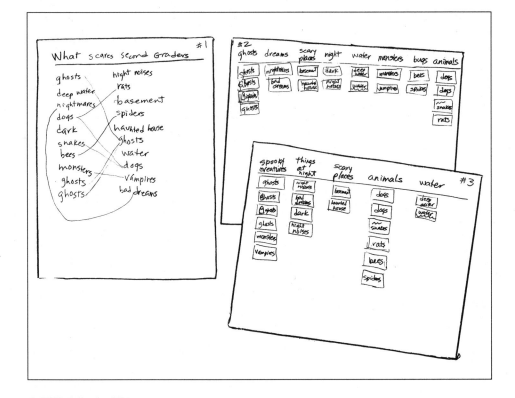

When students keep a succession of notes and drafts as they work, the teacher can follow the development of their mathematical thinking—as in this example from a data analysis project, where the students are finding ways to categorize their raw data meaningfully.

With younger students, work samples will involve less writing. Whatever their age, all students should be encouraged to record and represent their mathematical ideas, just as real mathematicians do. Even kindergartners can show—by drawing, pasting down stickers, or using other manipulatives—the number of apples of each color that were brought for the class fruit salad. When it's impractical to actually collect the students' constructions for examination (because they are too bulky, or because the students need to use the manipulatives again soon), it's easy enough to take snapshots of their work or to make a quick sketch. Having students make sketches of their own constructions is a great idea, too, as it prompts a whole new round of mathematical thinking: How do I transform this three-dimensional thing into a two-dimensional drawing?

If possible, teachers should try to collect different forms of student work throughout a project. This will give an indication of how well students are able to express their mathematical ideas through writing, representations, step-by-step drawings, models, and so forth. Consider, for example, an investigation for which students design and build small toys with interlocking cubes. Once they have finished, they draw diagrams to show other students how to build the toy and also write instruction booklets to accompany the diagrams. Students then trade drawings and instruction booklets, and other teams use their instructions to reconstruct the toy. The teacher who uses this activity has many forms of evidence to assess students' work: the actual construction (or a picture of it), the drawings students have made, their written instruction booklets, the success of the new team of toy-builders in using the instructions to make the toy, and the discussions between teams of toy-designers and toy-builders as they work to reconcile their differences.

In addition to gathering student work from larger projects, it is also important, at least occasionally, to collect work from shorter activities. This not only gets students into the habit of recording, representing, and writing about their work, it also provides more information about areas of difficulty for students. For just about any problem, students can both *show* and *write* how they did it, and these papers will document how they are thinking about a particular aspect of mathematics. While many students are initially reluctant to write down exactly how they are solving a problem, teachers and researchers who encourage frequent writing about problem solving have found that it helps students be more explicit and clearer mathematical thinkers (Burns, 1992).

Having to explain, with words and representations, how they worked through a problem also helps students learn an important lesson about mathematics: Mathematics is not an "either-you-know-it-or-you-don't" enterprise, but rather a discipline that involves creative ideas, false starts, following different paths, and working through ideas. As students gain confidence in themselves as mathematical thinkers, they will provide clearer and more thorough writing about their thinking. Think of how much more we can know about our students from this kind of writing than from a worksheet filled with routine calculations!

How to Interpret Assessment Results

How do we interpret and examine the evidence we get from checking in with students and from their written work? The process should be very similar to what we have learned to do with students' writing. With writing, we comment on how successful the student has been in communicating his or her ideas. We look for and comment on clarity, indicate where we are confused, point out parts that have been effective in communicating a certain feeling or idea, and share our general reactions to the piece. While we may note mistakes in grammar or spelling, this is not our major focus. The same should hold true with respect to mathematical work: The *quality* of mathematical reasoning is what we're looking for. Whether our assessment involves talking with individual students or reflecting on their written work in mathematics, we should consider and comment on the following:

- The extent to which the students' use of mathematics was effective in helping them solve a problem.
- The flexibility and appropriateness of the students' strategies for solving a problem.
- Whether the students make use of traditional algorithms, and if they can explain why they work.
- The extent to which the students' explanations, representations, or drawings of their solutions clearly communicate their mathematical thinking.
- The accuracy of the students' work.
- Whether the students were able to use "false starts" or mistakes in order to get on the right track.
- How the students used tools to solve a problem.

We are looking for evidence that students are making progress at the deepest level of mathematical understanding. In particular, we focus on whether students use mathematical strategies that make sense and that work for a given problem. Suppose the problem involves comparing two sets of objects—one numbering 46, the other 64—to see which set has more. A student who adds up all the objects in both sets is, quite simply, employing a strategy that doesn't work. This child either hasn't understood the problem or hasn't seen that comparison involves a process other than addition. A second student, who compares by "counting on" from 46 to 64 and keeping track of the number of numbers along the way, has a more effective strategy, one that shows understanding of the problem. A third student, who says "46, 56, 66, that's 20, take away 2 to get down to 64, that's 18," is employing an even more elegant strategy for figuring out the difference. In assessing students' thinking, we are looking for strategies that are above all *effective*, but also for strategies that show more efficiency and make use of more mathematical knowledge (in the case of the third student, knowledge of tens).

With this type of assessment, as we examine different pieces of student work, we are bound to notice some kinds of evidence that we weren't looking for. That's important. One piece of work may provide strong evidence that Dominic really doesn't understand a mathematical idea that we thought he did; another piece might show an unusual or elegant solution of Niki's that we want to share with the class; and still another piece may give us a sense of how interested or uninterested Jenna is in mathematics, or how confident Tony is in his strategies. All of this is important information in understanding our students and shaping what happens next in the classroom.

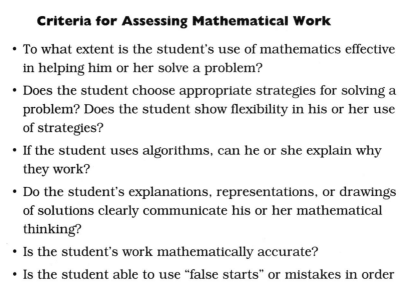

Criteria for Assessing Mathematical Work

- To what extent is the student's use of mathematics effective in helping him or her solve a problem?
- Does the student choose appropriate strategies for solving a problem? Does the student show flexibility in his or her use of strategies?
- If the student uses algorithms, can he or she explain why they work?
- Do the student's explanations, representations, or drawings of solutions clearly communicate his or her mathematical thinking?
- Is the student's work mathematically accurate?
- Is the student able to use "false starts" or mistakes in order to get on the right track?
- How does the student use tools to solve a problem?

How to Synthesize Assessment Information Over Time

At some point during the year, teachers need to synthesize all the information they are collecting. What does all of this assessment evidence mean about each student as a mathematical learner? We may know exactly how José makes his own representations of change (say, in plant growth) over time, how he demonstrates spatial strength in working with mapping problems, and how he uses the calculator to work with multiples. But what does all this tell us about José as a "whole" mathematical learner? The impetus for putting together the big picture may come from external sources, such as impending parent conferences, or decisions that need to be made about a student's class placement for next year. Or, it may come from the teacher's own questions about where to go next with a particular child. Regardless, at some point we'll want to systematically evaluate the evidence and come up with a composite picture.

Organizing Assessment Information

One helpful tool in organizing assessments and forming a composite picture of a child's mathematical work is the student portfolio. Although a great deal has been written about student portfolios (for example, Mumme, 1990; Stenmark, 1989), there are still many unresolved issues about how to make best use of portfolios in mathematics. A portfolio consists of samples of an individual's work collected over time. Its purpose is to convey a balanced, representative picture of that student's mathematical understanding. It is not an exhaustive, unwieldy collection of everything a student has done, but rather a selection of the student's best work, plus a sample of what the child has done with different kinds of mathematics problems and projects.

There are several major advantages to using portfolios. For one thing, they provide a variety of evidence of mathematical understanding and consequently are more valid than assessments relying on one kind of evidence. Further, they show quite clearly how the student's skills develop over time. Portfolios are also helpful in explaining to parents what kind of mathematics their child is doing, and how he or she is making sense of this mathematics. Finally, portfolios make sense logistically: Having completed work collected and organized for each student makes the whole evaluation process easier.

Despite the logistical advantages, most teachers find it quite difficult to begin using portfolios. A common mistake is collecting an overwhelming amount of work, only to be left with mountains of information to sort through and interpret. If you are new to math portfolios, ease into the process. You might first collect work for only a month or two, then examine it to determine what types of pieces have the most value for assessment. Or, you might start by collecting only an occasional piece of work from students. Here are some other ideas about getting started:

- Try to collect a sample of work that represents a student's understanding of different aspects of mathematics (for example, geometry, data, number). If you are working with a modular curriculum like *Investigations,* collect two to four pieces of work per unit to provide a broad picture of students' work across different areas of mathematics.

- Make sure the portfolio contains different types of work, including large projects and smaller ones, assignments that involve writing as well as those that do not, results of group work as well as individual work, and work that involves different kinds of representations (graphs, pictures, diagrams).

- Rote activities and conventional worksheets or textbook problems do not belong in a portfolio. The work that you collect should be meaningful, and should obviously involve some thought on the part of students.

- Many teachers feel that their reflections on a student's work (usually consisting of written feedback to the student) are another important part of the portfolio. Older students might want to include their own written reflections about the work they have done. If you are interested in more information on this reflection aspect of portfolios, see Ruth Parker's (1993) book *Mathematical Power* for an excellent example of a portfolio that shows real interaction between the teacher and student.

- Be sure to allow students some choice in what they put in their portfolio, and encourage them to bring in work that they've done outside of math class. Mathematical work that they've undertaken on their own—like figuring out win-loss records of their favorite teams, or calculating how long they have to save their allowance to buy that special game—is good evidence of mathematical thinking, as well as evidence that the students are making mathematics part of their lives.

- Last but not least, remember to have students put dates on all their work. It's frustrating to get to the end of a semester or year and not be able to reconstruct the order in which pieces were done.

Piecing Together the Bigger Picture

Once we have collected portfolios that contain representative examples of student work, we are ready to analyze this information. Just how we do this depends on our purpose. Some teachers go through the information before a parent conference and make notes about what they think the work demonstrates about the student's development. When parents come in, the teacher walks them through the portfolio, using the prepared notes to discuss the child's development and pointing out specific examples that illustrate progress. Other teachers use portfolios at the end of each grading period to put together a written narrative about each student's mathematical understanding. This narrative may be supplemented with copies of actual work. Following is an example of how one teacher used a third grader's portfolio to write a report about his skills and how they developed:

> Pierre started the year not being very sure about how to solve problems involving number. He tried unsuccessfully to remember how to carry and borrow, and frequently asked other children how to do these procedures.

> As the year progressed, Pierre grew more willing to use his own ideas for putting together and taking apart numbers. He learned to "find the tens." When combining numbers like 67 and 34, he'd first look to see how many obvious tens there were (the tens in 60 and 30), then he'd look for the tens that were "hiding," as he called it. He made this into a game, and soon expanded his skills by combining larger numbers, such as the number of children in all the classrooms at school. He began to seek out more challenging problems and made up a number of exciting number problems for himself and his friends.

> Pierre loved the units on geometry, and his map-reading interests and skills were something he enthusiastically shared with the rest of the class. He became an expert in giving directions for how to get around the school, and showed unusual skill in coordinating a series of directions involving turns and paces. His geometric reasoning, especially in this context, is flexible, focused, and sophisticated. However, he was reluctant to record his directions in a way that communicated fully to others. In general, recording and keeping track of his mathematical thinking is something that was difficult for Pierre, something we will continue to work on.

> Pierre initially showed less interest in the data projects than in other areas of mathematics, perhaps because he was reticent about gathering data from children he didn't know. However, when data-gathering involved scientific data, as in our "sink or

float" project, Pierre showed more interest and made some excellent observations about things that neither sink nor float. His classification of these "in-between" objects inspired his partners, and the representation his group made of their work was detailed, clear, and showed solid analytical skills.

Overall, Pierre shows strong mathematical skills and has made impressive gains in his confidence in dealing with numbers, particularly in his strategies for putting numbers together and taking them apart.

The report tells us a great deal about Pierre's thinking. The teacher has been selective in her use of evidence, and has certainly not told us everything that she knows about Pierre's mathematics. However, the examples she has chosen as well as the inferences she has drawn show how Pierre's mathematical thinking is evolving.

How to Explain Assessment Evidence to Parents

Even if we have managed to collect meaningful evidence about each student, to piece together this evidence into a coherent portrayal of the student's mathematical skills, and to demonstrate how the student's understanding of mathematics is progressing, our work is not done. We need to be able to communicate this evidence to parents— parents who may be expecting percentiles, test scores, and grades. Parents may come into a conference expecting these more traditional forms of evidence, and instead we show them pieces of their child's work with explanations of what it means, tell them how their child puzzles through problems of logic, and give them pictures of magnificent 3-D constructions made from blocks. Or, we may hand them a carefully written report of the child's mathematical understanding, like the report about Pierre.

How do parents react? Some will be most appreciative. When a teacher respects each student enough to examine, understand, and explain his or her strengths and weaknesses, some parents sense that they are receiving an unusual gift. It is as if the teacher had worked many months to paint a sensitive portrait of their child, one that reflects the many aspects of the child's mathematical intellect.

It need not be the teacher's responsibility alone to compose this portrait. Some teachers are experimenting with having the students themselves "present" what they are learning mathematically (Parker, 1993; Hart, 1994). The children may write letters to their parents, introducing their mathematics portfolios and commenting on the most important things they have learned. Or, the students can appear as partners with the teacher during parent conferences, sharing what they are learning, showing the work they are especially proud of, and talking with pride about their progress. Involving students in communicating about the results of assessment encourages them to articulate what is important mathematically and to take greater responsibility for their learning. At the same time, it gives parents a direct link to what their children are doing mathematically and encourages families to talk together about mathematics.

Questions That Parents Frequently Ask

It should not be surprising that many parents are unfamiliar with new forms of assessment. Teachers will need to explain how assessment is now focused on students' strategies rather than on answers alone, and how it aims to examine a deeper level of mathematical understanding. Parents typically have some questions about their children's skills that teachers should be prepared to address:

☞ **How is my child doing compared to everyone else in the class? Is she average or above average? Is she lagging behind?**

Parents often want to know not only how their child is doing in mathematics, but how well she is doing *relative to others*. They are naturally concerned about how well their child will "make it" in the world. Some parents who ask these questions are really seeking assurance that their child is bright enough to make it into a selective college many years from now, while others just want to know if their child is performing at grade level or trying hard enough in class. Some want to know if their child needs additional help. Discerning the nature of parents' questions can help us answer them. Part of our explanation will focus on the fact that math (or any other subject area) has many dimensions, and that their child has real strengths in some of these dimensions, but is struggling with others. While parents love to learn about their child's strengths, we also need to let them know when their child is having problems mathematically, to explain what we are doing to help, and let parents know if there's anything they can do at home.

Part of the problem when we describe children's strengths in a qualitative, descriptive way, is that parents do not have a framework for interpreting the information. *We* see Eleanor in class every day, and *we* have a sense of how she does mathematics relative to the rest of the class. Eleanor's parents, on the other hand, see only *her* math work—not that of her peers. They may see that she has very unusual strategies for dividing, that she thinks about fractions by drawing them, and that she doesn't respond very quickly when they ask her to do multiplication problems. Their question about "how is she doing?"—sometimes followed by a question about whether you have standardized test scores for Eleanor—may be a plea for help in interpreting their daughter's mathematical skills. They need to hear us explain that her "unusual" strategies are actually very strong and effective (or, that these strategies *aren't* working for her); they need to know that her drawings of fractions mean she's using spatial skills to figure out fractions, and that this strategy is (or is not) leading to improvement in her skills.

Beyond simply explaining to parents, there are many ways we can demonstrate where their child stands. During a conference, we can walk through the classroom with parents and point out examples of student work. This way parents can see for themselves how their son's geometric constructions or number patterns relate to those made by other children in the class. Sometimes we may even want to encourage parents to observe in the classroom during math class, paying particular attention to their own child's mathematical strategies in relation to those of other children. By making the classroom mathematics community more visible and accessible to parents, we allow them to see where their child fits in this community.

Here's another piece of this problem: When teachers are using a new curriculum and a new form of assessment, it's harder for *them* to confidently explain how any one student is doing relative to his or her peers. There are no percentiles or stanines to point to—and even though these traditional test scores can be misleading, they at least inspired confidence in parents, who saw standardized tests as objective, scientific measures of their child's mathematical thinking. Teachers may feel uncomfortable about having little objective evidence—a discomfort that often comes with the transition to a new way of teaching. They need opportunities to see many different students working through their own strategies before they can tell where a particular child might be going next or how mathematically sound his or her approaches are.

If you're new at the constructivist approach, give yourself time to collect evidence about the students in your class, to compare the effectiveness of different students' approaches, and to develop your own ways of analyzing mathematical thinking. In the meantime, show parents evidence from portfolios of how their child is developing mathematically. Invite them to observe for themselves the mathematical work that their child—and the rest of the class—is doing.

☛ **How is my child at computation? Should I be doing more workbook math with him to improve his computational skills?**

Communicating to parents how their child handles computation is important, because computation is a key and widely recognized piece of mathematics. We need to keep some samples of students' strategies as they play number games, solve comparison problems, or work on multiplication arrays. If parents tell us that their child does not "know" her multiplication tables (or some other kind of facts), this is exactly the right moment to bring up Natalie's marvelous skill in using what she knows about the number system to deal with a series of related multiplication problems. We can tell how Natalie did $9 \times 6 = 54$ by reasoning this way: "I know that 10 sixes is 60, but I only have 9 sixes, so it must be 6 less, so 54." This took Natalie only a few seconds to figure out, and showed that she has done much more than just memorize—she understands how to use her knowledge of tens to derive new relationships.

Teachers using a constructivist curriculum should expect to reassure parents that it's a good thing for their child to do computation in unusual ways. Parents need to understand that children's own strategies are often much better than the "recipes" because, when memory fails them, children still have a way of figuring out how to do problems. We should be prepared to give examples of how Omar's strategies work for him. Or, if Omar is bound to the algorithm and not developing his own strategies, we can explain to his parents how we'd like him to develop his problem-solving skills. Using workbooks or flash cards should be discouraged. Instead, we can suggest games the family can play at home to reinforce their child's own ways of adding, subtracting, multiplying, and dividing. A book like Peggy Kaye's (1987) *Games for Math* is worth recommending, as are many of the games included in a constructivist curriculum like *Investigations.*

Questions You May Not Hear, But Ought to Address

Following are some questions we wish we heard more often from parents. Even if we *don't* hear these questions, we can plan to address some of them anyway, with the aim of describing the multifaceted nature of a child's mathematical understanding.

- How is my child doing with geometry and spatial relationships?
- Does my child show that she links her knowledge of the real world to her knowledge of mathematics?
- Does my child understand data and how to use it?
- Does my child understand that how he solves a problem is more important than the answer itself?
- Does my child love doing math and see herself as a competent mathematician?
- Does my child hold his own in mathematical discussions, or does he defer to other students?

It probably isn't possible—or necessary—to comment on all of these questions for each child. But if we bring some of these nontraditional issues into our conferences with parents, we'll be helping them learn what real mathematics is all about and how they can help their child learn it.

How to Deal With Standardized Tests

In many schools, teachers are required to administer standardized tests. These tests are a very poor gauge of mathematical understanding, as has been discussed extensively by researchers and policymakers (NCTM, 1995; Schwartz, 1992; Kamii, 1990; National Center for Fair and Open Testing, 1991). The weaknesses of these tests include the following:

- Standardized tests focus heavily on timed computation, while this skill is one that should receive decreased emphasis, according to NCTM.

- Most standardized tests put a premium on rote knowledge and memorization.

- Most standardized tests do not require students to show their thinking or strategies, nor do they assign a higher score for better strategies.

- Many test questions are devoid of context, or have contexts that are inaccessible to some students (particularly girls and students whose primary language is not English).

- Most tests allow for only one correct response to a question, while there may be several ways of perceiving a problem.

A single example can demonstrate some of the flaws in standardized tests. During a research project on the impact of the *Investigations* curriculum, we administered several traditional test items to fourth graders to see how they would do. One of the items was 34 ÷ 8. A student came up to the tester and said that she could not do the problem because there wasn't enough information. "What do you mean?" asked the tester. The girl replied, "I need to know what kind of things the 34 are. Are they things like cookies that can be divided into fractions in the end, or are they things like balloons, where you can't divide them into fractions?" The tester suggested that she do the problem both ways. The student showed her work and came up with two answers: 4 and $1/4$, and 4 with 2 extra. By contrast, most of the children who had experienced a traditional fourth grade curriculum wrote simply "4 R 2." None used fractions. Yet, on a standardized test, the girl who had two answers may well have "incorrectly" filled in "none of the above" on her multiple choice response blank, because she was not satisfied with the standard answer. This example shows how inadequate standardized tests can be in capturing real understanding.

Testing problems like these crop up more often as children become sophisticated mathematical problem solvers. Despite these inadequacies, teachers are still stuck with tests. Many worry how their students will do on these tests if they haven't been drilled extensively on traditional math content. Sometimes, the tests carry high stakes; they may be used to compare the performance of various schools, or even to evaluate teacher effectiveness. The misuses of tests are real, and it is important that teachers do what they can to educate administrators, parents, and each other about the limitations of these tests. While we may not be able to eliminate the tests overnight, we can aim to educate others about the fact that the tests do not measure the important mathematical skills that our students need. The following facts and resources can bolster such efforts:

- The National Association for the Education of Young Children (NAEYC) has concluded that standardized testing is actually harmful for young children and has strongly recommended that no child younger than fourth grade be subjected to any form of standardized testing (Kamii, 1990).

- The nationwide New Standards Project (Daro, 1993) is developing a new assessment program that consists *solely* of meaningful mathematics tasks that require students to spend substantial time on a small number of challenging problems. There will be no timed calculation, and students will be encouraged to use calculators and other tools. In many states, this new assessment will totally replace standardized tests. In fact, at this writing, 19 states have already agreed to use the new tests to replace traditional ones (Andy Plattner, Communications Director, National Center on Education and the Economy, personal communication, 1994). Any school not preparing its students to develop mathematical thinking skills will be at a serious disadvantage when this assessment is implemented on a wide-scale basis.

- The National Council of Teachers of Mathematics, in its new *Assessment Standards for School Mathematics* (1995), is recommending that traditional standardized tests be totally eliminated over the next several years. They contend that current tests are simply not compatible with reform goals in mathematics education, and they endorse the new alternative assessments such as those being developed by the New Standards Project.

Fortunately, even in a school that's stuck with standardized testing, there's no reason for teachers to panic or to change their curriculum in order to prepare students for the tests. As mentioned in chapter 4, research is increasingly showing that students in a constructivist mathematics curriculum do just as well on untimed tests of computation as do students exposed to a more traditional curriculum—and they typically do better on the applications and concepts sections of these tests (Abruscato, 1993). Our own research with third graders has shown that, over the academic year, students who participated in the *Investigations* curriculum improved their computational skills, as did the students in traditional classes. The gains were roughly equal—though students in the *Investigations* group were more likely to use their own strategies, rather than the standard procedures, for doing computations involving multiplication, addition, subtraction, and division. *Investigations* students sometimes gave more thorough responses, while students in a traditional curriculum gave one standard response. We must have faith in the strategies children develop on their own—they don't need a uniform procedure in order to perform well on tests.

Some teachers have coped with the testing dilemma by spending a couple of class periods before the test coaching their students on what to expect, and helping them make links between what they know and what's likely to be on the test. For example, imagine a class of students who have been studying division at a fairly deep level—like the girl who, when asked to solve 34 ÷ 8, wanted to know "34 of *what?*" These students have discovered that when working with some kinds of objects (like balloons), it makes sense to distribute whole numbers of things and simply put the leftovers off to one side. With objects like cookies, it might make sense to divide the leftovers into fractional pieces and distribute these evenly. The students in this class, while having a very sophisticated notion of division, may not know about the "official" way of indicating remainders. It is easy enough to explain that R 2 is the way of showing that we have two balloons left over once we divide up all the balloons.

We can also take a few minutes to explain the peculiar conventions of standardized tests—multiple-choice format, timing, only one correct answer. This way students will know that the test is a unique situation where their usual ways of doing mathematics need to be adapted.

Finally, we can let students know that while they need to try their best, we value all the other mathematical work they have done more than we value their test scores. Maintaining students' mathematical self-esteem throughout the testing process is the critical goal.

CHAPTER 6

Finding Time and a Place for Math

Most elementary school teachers in this country spend only about three hours a day altogether on "core" subject areas such as reading and writing, history, and mathematics—and they spend less than an hour a day on mathematics instruction (*Prisoners of Time*, 1994). Students are simply not studying mathematics as much as they need to be. They cannot be expected to become fluent in mathematics if they spend the typical 140 hours a year or less doing it. Many children spend far more than 140 hours a year participating in sports or music, and most of them spend over 700 hours a year watching TV (U.S. Dept. of Education, 1994). Certainly mathematical fluency, given its importance in a child's future, deserves as much time and attention as extracurricular activities.

In U.S. schools, unlike those in Europe or Asia, there is a lack of balance in the time spent on academic subject areas. In other countries, roughly equal emphasis is placed on mathematics and language arts. In contrast, American elementary school teachers spend the bulk of their time on language arts—reading, writing, phonics, spelling, and grammar—and devote proportionately less time to mathematics. The emphasis on language is further enhanced in public messages: Parents are encouraged by everyone from teachers to TV actors to Barbara Bush to "read to your child," but there is no equivalent public awareness campaign in mathematics. The net effect is that children spend a significant amount of time inside and outside the classroom on language arts, and a much lesser amount of time on mathematics.

There is no doubt that mathematical literacy is a worthy goal, and one that needs more emphasis in schools. But if teachers spend more time on mathematics, what sacrifices do they make in the rest of the curriculum? How can more mathematics be packed into an already overwhelming schedule? Recently, the National Education Commission on Time and Learning recommended that U.S. schools double the amount of time spent on core areas such as mathematics (*Prisoners of Time*, 1994). According to their recommendations, this would be accomplished by "reclaiming" the school day for academic instruction, lengthening the school day, and lengthening the school year. In the long run, said the commission, we must "reinvent schools around learning, not time" (p. 30).

The debate about how much time should be spent in school has just begun, and it is unlikely that the school schedule will change radically in the near future. Meanwhile, teachers need some arguments and strategies for incorporating more mathematics into children's lives. We can take simultaneous action on three fronts: (1) doing more mathematics in regular classroom time; (2) increasing the visibility of and emphasis on mathematics in the school; and (3) promoting mathematics education among families, in the same way that reading education is currently being promoted.

Getting More Math Into the Classroom

Given the importance of mathematics, it is essential that teachers devote a minimum of an hour of each classroom day to this subject. In fact, students need solid blocks of time, often longer than an hour, to study mathematics. And they need to do math every day, just as they read every day. While scheduling longer math classes is a start, there are many other ways to spend more time on mathematics throughout the day. Following are some suggestions.

Include Mathematics in Interdisciplinary Projects

While mathematics is a core subject area in and of itself, it is also intertwined with and enhances other disciplines. Constructivist mathematics develops both written and oral communication skills and necessitates critical thinking and logic. Students must learn how to argue on the basis of evidence, to show how they discovered a solution, and to convince others of their logic by using words, tools, and effective displays. In working through a problem, students must listen to each other and try to understand approaches other than their own. They learn that talking about, writing about, and considering different ways into a problem makes the problem easier to solve. All these skills cross disciplinary boundaries and are worth taking the time to cultivate. In doing math, students simultaneously accomplish many other learning goals. Two examples of projects in the *Investigations* curriculum demonstrate the ways mathematics can interact with the much bigger realm of social science, science, and literacy skills.

Playground injuries.   In a data investigation, fifth graders conduct their own research about school and playground injuries. Through surveys, observations, and even reviews of existing records, students determine what types of injuries occur and how these injuries are related to different activities (organized sports, using playground equipment), to different places (inside school, blacktop area, field), and to different ages. Their goal is to identify injury "hot spots," and to use their evidence to make recommendations about how to alleviate the problems they've identified.

One of the early field tests of this investigation took place in a classroom at Central Park East (one of the New York City Public Schools) where fifth graders examined injury data carefully over a period of time. They discovered that more injuries took place as crowding increased on the playground, and that fewer injuries took place when more adults were present. They wrote about their findings, and the class developed a set of recommendations that they presented to the principal. Students had some excellent suggestions about scheduling recess time differently so that there would be less crowding. They also had some ideas about maximizing the adult supervision that was available and concentrating it in areas where it was most needed. The principal was genuinely impressed with the data-gathering and use of evidence to formulate a plan for improvement and was able to implement some of the students' suggestions.

Through this investigation, the teacher engaged his fifth graders in social studies, writing, mathematics, community service, oral communication, and even epidemiology. Mathematics expanded into other times of the day, and it indeed shaped what happened during writing and social studies class. But far from getting in the way of learning about other disciplines, this mathematics project enhanced the relevance of learning in other areas. The goal of this project—writing and communicating about real findings for a real audience—contributed as much to the students' mathematical development as it did to the development of literacy and community service skills.

A trip around the United States.   As part of their study of large numbers, fourth graders plan a trip around the United States that will take them to 4–10 different places, with a total mileage log of less than 10,000 miles. In this investigation, students learn how to combine and compare large numbers: "We've been to 6 places and traveled 9,260 miles. Can we still travel to Pittsburgh and keep our total miles under 10,000?" Moreover, they learn how to read maps, use scales, estimate distances, and identify places in the country they'd like to visit.

In classrooms that are willing to spend the time on interdisciplinary work, this investigation builds stronger social studies and science skills through extensions that involve the study of famous journeys. For example, some classrooms have extended the basic trip-planning activity by studying and plotting the journeys of enslaved people attempting to get to freedom. Others have retraced the journeys of immigrant groups, or even people within their own families who have come from other countries. Still other classrooms have linked the mathematics of travel with the study of bird or butterfly migration. Through this mathematical investigation, then, students can also discover a great deal about geography, the history of slavery or immigration, or the nature of animal migration.

In these two examples, mathematics takes a *leading* role in the interdisciplinary project. Too often, interdisciplinary investigations put math in the role of supporting actor; in many cases, the mathematics is merely tacked on in an unmeaningful way. Students deserve to hear a different message about mathematics, and mathematics deserves the starring role in at least some interdisciplinary investigations.

Solve Everyday Classroom Problems by Using Mathematics

A second strategy for infusing more mathematics into the regular classroom day is to recognize and act upon the mathematical opportunities that come up daily. As teachers, we solve mathematical problems all the time. For example, this morning the class needs to be at music by 10:30, and you've just started math, which lasts about one hour. There's a video you want to show that lasts 25 minutes. Is there time for it? Why not give this and other classroom mathematical problems to the students to solve? We've been doing this for decades by milking the mathematics out of lunch money, but it's worth expanding upon these mathematical opportunities.

With lunch money, there's a predictable need to count the children who are buying lunch in the cafeteria, to figure out how much money should be collected to buy these lunches, to count the money, and to determine whether it's the right amount. Students have many ingenious ways of doing this—none of them necessarily the way that the teacher would do it. As long as the strategy accomplishes the goal, the students are engaged in good mathematics.

Similarly, young students have many different ways of solving attendance problems. Finding out how many are absent on a given day is not a cut-and-dried problem for young children. Some may simply name and count the number of children who are not there, while others may insist that this is not a reliable way of taking attendance. These doubters may come up with the strategy of counting the total number of students currently in the room and comparing it to the number of names on the class list. Comparing the 19 students in the room with the 27 on the class list is not a trivial mathematical task for the early grades, and it's an important one that predictably arises each day.

Throughout the year, comparing the number of students present with the total number in the class continues to be a meaningful problem. As the year progresses, the students also might look for patterns in their attendance data: Are there times of the week or month when most or all of them are present? Times when a lot of them are absent? What's the usual number of students present in class? Daily problems like these can be embellished as the year goes on and as the students' mathematical sophistication increases.

Whenever we find ourselves doing a practical mathematical problem, we need to stop and consider whether the class might assume some ownership of it. Obviously, problems need to be geared to the developmental level of the children, but a vast range of everyday problems will be accessible. For example, at different levels, both younger and older children can help figure out how many parent drivers are needed for a class trip. In this situation, young children can deal with this problem: "We have 3 drivers so far, and we need 7 altogether.

How many more drivers do we need?" Older students can deal with more complicated questions, taking into account how many seats are available in each parent's car and the implications for how many vehicles are needed.

The more that we involve children in solving everyday mathematical problems, the less likely they are to raise those pesky and all-too-familiar questions, "Why do we need to learn this? What are we ever going to use it for?"

Do More Math During "Down" Time

All of us have more than our share of "down" time—the times when the class is lining up, when the assembly has been delayed, or when it's indoor recess again. While most teachers have good games in their repertoires to deal with these down times, how often do we think of using the time for mathematics? In some of the new constructivist mathematics curricula, there are short activities that specifically address these needs. Often these are mental math activities that can be done just about anywhere—things like estimating the number of seats in the auditorium where you're waiting for the play to begin, or the time-honored game of Guess My Rule (an example follows). One appealing characteristic of these activities is that little preparation is needed. Another plus is that you can do the activities over and over, with minor variations, without losing students' attention.

Here are just a few examples of how teachers might capitalize on mathematics during spare moments or down time:

- It's indoor recess and the first graders are restless. It's a perfect time for an active round of Guess My Rule. In today's version of the game, the teacher asks each student to take off one shoe and then begins sorting the shoes into two groups. When one child asks what's going on, the teacher announces, "I have a rule to explain how I'm sorting these shoes. Give me your shoe and tell me which group you think it goes in." As the game progresses, students begin to guess the teacher's rule, eliminating possible rules based on the feedback they get about where the shoes belong. Later they play the game again, trying to guess a student's rule.

- The second graders are lining up for the bus. The teacher asks, "If we count by threes down this line of kids who are waiting for the bus, what number will we end up with?" The students begin to count off, each saying the next number in sequence: 3, 6, 9, 12, and so forth. The teacher stops them when they are halfway down the line and asks for a new prediction concerning what number they will end up with.

- Fourth graders are putting away their writing materials and waiting to go to lunch. One student comments that they still have 3 minutes before the bell. The teacher asks, "How many seconds is that? How many seconds would it be if you had to wait 5 minutes? 10 minutes? a whole hour?"

Fitting more mathematics into down time does necessitate a little planning. It means having a repertoire of quick math games and activities available, and choosing an activity that will match students' moods, interests, and level of energy. It also means changing children's expectations about when and where mathematics happens. An important message to communicate is that students don't need to "veg out" or simply wait around for the next activity; they can do some productive math instead, and at the same time have fun.

Going After Increased Visibility

One way of getting more time devoted to mathematics is to make it more visible on a schoolwide basis. Focusing attention on the role of mathematics in the school means creating events, programs, and displays that draw students, teachers, parents, and administrators into mathematics. Most elementary schools sponsor several special events and programs that involve science, language arts, music, or the visual arts. Even spelling has its spelling bees. While these programs vary in quality and the kinds of messages that are conveyed, the point is that they generate schoolwide interest and attention. They also legitimize and emphasize the importance of spending substantial amounts of in- and out-of-class time on the subject area.

Science fairs offer an interesting model. Before a science fair, teachers and students from all participating classes are busily engaged in selecting appropriate experiments, gathering data, modifying and repeating scientific procedures, and determining clear and engaging ways of representing results. In many schools, students work together on their science projects in small groups and spend considerable time creating, discussing, revising, and reflecting on their work. (These cooperative investigations are generally more effective than the kind of fairs that pit students against each other in competition.) The resulting "event" is a way for the school to demonstrate what is valued about science and how students at the school learn science. Also important, the students are provided with a real audience for their work. They must know their project intimately, because they must explain it to others.

Whenever an event like this occurs in any subject area, it is a way for teachers to communicate about educational values. It is a time for teachers to show that they value the process of doing real, intellectual work, complete with false starts, revisions, risk taking, and mistake making. It is a way for students to demonstrate the power of *how* they are learning.

Events such as these are rare occurrences in mathematics. It's hard to even imagine what a mathematics fair might look like. The closest we come in math are "junior college bowl" contests in which a small group of self-selected students competes. Often these contests do little more than take traditional math questions and translate them into a quiz format. Unfortunately, such events reinforce the myth that speed and accuracy are of utmost importance in math; they also suggest that "you either know math or you don't." When math is learned in a constructivist way, this kind of contest will not suffice as a way of demonstrating mathematical skill. But how can we give all students an audience and the opportunity to show their mathematical stuff? How can we provide them with meaningful opportunities to work on sustained projects that will of necessity involve a chunk of their free time? If we could think of more ways of doing this, we would also be showing the larger community the excitement and power of real mathematical thinking.

The Mathematician's Chair

One suggestion for getting started is to hold an event that's the mathematical equivalent of "author's chair." The basic concept behind this event is that students who have finished writing a story can sign up to read it aloud at the next "author's chair." Usually, several students sign up for the same event and take turns reading their stories. Once each author has read, the audience has a chance to ask questions about it ("Why did you make the main character be so nice to everyone?") and to share their reactions ("I really liked the way you solved the mouse's problem in the end"). Teachers who have held "author's chair" for sharing writing projects find that it is an excellent way for many children to communicate their writing to the broader community, including students from other classes, teachers, and parents.

Why not translate this concept to "mathematician's chair"? A student or group of students who have completed a significant piece of mathematical work are eligible to present it at this special event. They display work that represents the mathematics they've done and explain to an audience the strategies they used to solve the problem. The advantage of this type of event is that it is based on the work already being done by the class, and while it involves some preparation by the students, it can be kept low-key and fun. All students would be expected to participate at least once during the year.

Some teachers have held a "mathematician's chair" as a special event at the culmination of project work. For example, at the end of a computer investigation involving the activity "Geo-Face," third graders in one class were very curious about the faces they and others had constructed on the computer (Clements et al., 1995). The teacher found a time for them to share their work with each other and with students in another class, and asked students to sign up to present what they had constructed. She made a computer available to students, provided some time for them to prepare, and gave them a few suggestions about what they might present. For example:

• Choose one part of your face and explain how you made the perimeter of this part come out to the specified number.

• On the computer, show one procedure you used for making a face part.

- Tell about one problem you ran into when you were making your face, and explain how you solved it.

- Describe how you changed your plans for your face parts when you found they didn't work the way you thought they would.

"Mathematician's chair" is an event that can be held with a small audience of peers or with a larger audience that includes more people from outside the classroom. It is also quite possible to transform such an event into a bigger math fair by having several students "chairing" different presentations in different parts of the room. Visitors then stop in at several stations and have an opportunity to see and hear about several different math projects. Whatever the format, it's important to give students the responsibility for planning their presentation and deciding how to best communicate their strategies and what they learned.

Public Displays

Interactive hallway displays are another special way to demonstrate mathematical thinking to the broader community. With this kind of exhibition, students both show their work and encourage others to participate. For example, one classroom of first graders made a time line showing the current year, how long ago they were born, and marking other special events that had occurred at their school. Their time line was quite ambitious, being long enough to show the birth years of the teachers. In fact, the students found that the only place with enough room to display their long time line was the cafeteria. After it was exhibited there, the class quickly discovered that others were not only interested in their work, they had spontaneously added their own important dates to the time line.

At that point, the first graders added a sign that encouraged others—especially teachers—to fill in their own birth year data and information about the school's history. Because the display was in the cafeteria, students who had finished eating lunch early often spent considerable time studying the time line and adding information to it. They were often overheard trying to figure out the ages of teachers who were born "in the olden days" (the 1950s). By sharing their time line with others and inviting others to contribute to it, this group of young students sparked considerable interest in mathematics in their school. Over a couple of weeks, almost everyone at the school spent at least a few minutes perusing the time line and figuring out problems that were of interest to them.

The time line example is of special interest because it was a significant, quiet, and easy way of promoting more mathematical problem solving within the school. The display engaged teachers as well as students. A few teachers decided that they would try a similar activity in their own classrooms. The teacher of the first graders had not intended to involve the entire community in mathematical discussions about birth years, but this is what happened when the students' work went public.

People can't help but notice when students are either showing or doing their mathematical work in a public place. One principal, after seeing a group of third graders spend a few days measuring the distances between places in the school, commented that "everyone who walked by wanted to know what the kids were doing. And everyone had their predictions about what distances were farthest. You could not avoid the mathematics that was happening in that hallway, because you were practically tripping over it."

Working With Other Classrooms

It's not always necessary to have special events or displays to involve the broader community in mathematical thinking. Many mathematical investigations require getting input or data from another classroom. For example, in the activity "Nobody There," young students are asked to figure out how many students are in another classroom in the school—when the class is not there. They have to decide which things to count in order to figure out the population of this room. Will chairs do it? How about coats, or lunch boxes? Counts of different objects may yield different results, and students need to decide which count would be more accurate. Once students have made the decision, they bring the necessary number of cookies (or some other treat) to the neighboring classroom. They also bring a description of how they estimated the number of children in the class, and check out their estimate with the class. One letter, dictated to the teacher by kindergartners, went like this:

Dear Ms. Stephano's class:

We went to your room to count how many kids there were while you were gone. It was a secret. We wanted to surprise you with cookies, and we needed to know how many to bring. David and Enrico counted chairs and thought there were 24 kids in your room. Josie and Kym counted lunch boxes and there were only 22. Some other kids counted cubbies and there were 23, but one was empty and others had letters in them. Most of us thought there were 22 kids in your class. You might have a couple of extra chairs. Were we right?

For the school as a community, the value of cross-classroom investigations is that they involve a broader group in real mathematical and social questions, while also giving other teachers a sense of the interesting mathematics that is going on in their school.

It's entirely possible that the best way of convincing our colleagues of the value of constructivist mathematics is by letting the students' work speak for itself and generate excitement. In the effort to change the mathematics culture at a school, a single teacher may not have nearly the impact of an enthusiastic group of student mathematicians.

In fact, students can do a great deal to increase the visibility of mathematics among audiences ranging from their own parents to school board members. One California teacher, who wanted to convince her school board to commit funds to a new constructivist math curriculum, had two of her fifth graders attend a board meeting and demonstrate various ways they could divide a rectangle into thirds. They even had board members try the activity of finding "weird thirds" on the paper equivalent of a geoboard. The teacher who organized this presentation knew that having the children themselves articulate and engage in a meaningful mathematical problem—and inviting the audience to engage in the problem—would be a powerful, concrete way of demonstrating the nature of the reform movement in mathematics.

If we can find opportunities like these for students to show and write about their mathematical work, we will be providing them an audience, giving them a chance to spend more time doing mathematics, and at the same time furthering our efforts toward reform.

Promoting Math to Parents

Making mathematics more visible within a school has the valuable side effect of modeling for parents and families the kind of mathematics that happens at school. Special events and displays are a way for children to show their parents their mathematical work and to prompt discussion about this work. It is imperative that we find more ways of encouraging parents to talk and do mathematics with their children, just as they read with them. Unfortunately, getting the message across to parents will certainly be harder with math than with reading. Most parents, like the rest of us, have rather impoverished mathematical backgrounds. While many parents read magazines and books on occasion (both on their own and with their children), far fewer do any mathematics that is visible to their children. Parents remember the drudgery of school math and may well have negative attitudes toward it. Even if they know mathematics is important to their children's futures, they probably don't know what they can do about it at home.

Teachers face two types of difficulties in working with parents. One problem is that many families simply don't support their children's mathematical learning at home, perhaps because they don't know how, or because they lack the time. The other difficulty teachers encounter is with parents who are strong supporters of *traditional* mathematics learning and do not understand how constructivist mathematics will benefit their children. These parents may be spending time doing mathematics with their children at home, but they are using workbooks and flash cards rather than meaningful mathematics activities. These parents have not experienced good mathematics themselves, and all they can teach their children is what they know. In both cases, working successfully with families will necessitate *communicating* about and *demonstrating* to parents what is happening in mathematics class. At the same time, teachers need to model and explicitly suggest ways that good mathematics can happen at home.

Letters and Visits

Communication with families needs to be regular and ongoing. Parents should hear about upcoming units of study or special mathematics activities, along with ideas for what they can do at home to supplement what is happening in class. Many new mathematics curricula provide letters to families that help teachers explain what will be happening in the classroom and enlist parental support. Often, these letters are provided in different languages to assist teachers who work with different language groups. Whether teachers use these standard letters or write their own, the important thing is to say in clear, straightforward language what mathematics is being addressed, why it is important, and what home activities can be done to support this learning. Some teachers also like to share interesting classroom mathematics anecdotes in these letters—readers are likely to pay more attention when there's the possibility that their own children will appear in these stories!

Another part of ongoing communication is pointing out the mathematics that is happening in the classroom when parents have occasion to visit, or when they stop by to pick up their children at the end of the day. These visits are an opportunity for parents to link what they read about in the letters with what their child is doing. For example, it only takes a minute to say to a parent, "Check Alicia's math journal from yesterday. She made some interesting drawings that show how she understands fractions." Similarly, it's easy to direct a parent's attention to a new display of the students' graphs, or to their paper constructions of geometric shapes. In this way, a teacher can connect the "telling" in the letters that go home with the "showing" of student work.

Parent Conferences

Parent conferences, which often happen at the beginning or end of the school year, are the most obvious show-and-tell mechanism available to teachers. In these conferences, it is important to link the how and what of the mathematics curriculum with a child's actual work. Talking to a parent about the geometry curriculum may sound vague and abstract—until we bring out the pop-up constructions and show how their child has learned to transform two-dimensional paper into three-dimensional displays. Unless the teacher points it out, the parent may not realize that these constructions represent important geometric learning—to a parent, they look like an art project. Conferences are also a good time to link home and school mathematics learning. If a child has been searching for and identifying *shapes* at home, this is the chance to talk about how it relates to the "Shape Hunt" that was done in class. The conferences are a way of helping parents make connections between pieces of their child's learning that may seem disparate.

Some teachers use conferences as a way for students themselves to communicate with their parents. Sometimes the students write a preconference letter to their parents about the mathematical work in their portfolio, maybe pointing out a mathematical piece that they are especially proud of, or telling what they hope to learn. Such letters give the children a chance to articulate the mathematics they are doing. In some cases, older elementary school students actually participate in the conference, explaining to their parents what they are doing in mathematics class, what is important and interesting about it, and what is difficult. When a child talks about and shows his or her mathematical work, parents will take notice. They are then more likely to know how to start a mathematical conversation with their child—a conversation based on the actual work their child is doing. During the conference, the teacher can also *model* for parents how to carry on mathematical discussions—listening carefully to what the child has to say and raising questions that will lead to more in-depth mathematical thinking.

Math Curriculum Night

If a teacher is working with lots of parents who are used to traditional math and don't understand why this year's class is different, it can be valuable to stage a math curriculum night. This gives parents the chance to ask questions about the curriculum, and gives teachers the chance to show the curriculum in action. In some cases, an entire school—or all the classes at one grade level—may sponsor a math curriculum meeting; in other cases, one teacher may do it alone. Formats for these meetings vary considerably; the main point is that parents have ample opportunity to ask questions and to see the actual work that students are doing. Following are some possibilities for a good parent meeting:

Videotapes.   A good introduction for a meeting is one of two videotapes: (1) *What Are You Teaching My Child?*—a Marilyn Burns (1994) video, specifically for parents, which introduces the idea of constructivist math and demonstrates concretely why children need math to prepare for their futures; or (2) *Math Matters: Kids Are Counting On You*—another videotape for parents developed by The National PTA (1989), which explains how and why mathematics education is changing.

A quiz.   The *Math Matters* package contains a good quiz about common math myths. Teachers who do not choose to show the tape may still want to use the quiz and discuss which statements are true and which are false. This will help parents better understand the role of mathematics in their children's future.

Parent problem-solving activity.   A good way of showing parents what's different about today's mathematics is to have them work together on a meaty but nonthreatening problem, one that takes some thought. A good problem will have several different solutions or several different ways of arriving at the answer. There's an interesting problem about horse-trading in the Burns videotape: "A man buys a horse for $50, sells it for $60, buys it back for $70, and sells it again for $80. How much money did the man gain or lose?"

Another type of problem involves making estimates and discussing estimation strategies. For example: "About how many bicycles do you think are owned by all the families whose children attend this school?" Here, the exact answer is not known, but many important statistical assumptions go into solving the problem. Parents will probably decide on different techniques for estimating the population of the school, determining how many families are in the school, and determining how many bicycles there are per family (given the likely age range and fitness levels of people in the families). Sharing strategies for addressing the problem helps parents understand what is involved in mathematical thinking—and since there is no "right" answer, the problem is not threatening. Whatever the problem, the point is to give parents a firsthand feel for doing mathematics a different way.

A self-guided classroom tour.   As parents arrive in the classroom, they pick up an annotated list of different places in the room where mathematical work is on display. One stop may be their own child's math journal or portfolio; another may be a wall display of data; yet another, a tabletop collection of children's symmetrical pattern-block designs. One especially good stop is a display of homework (which parents may have seen their children doing), with a clear link to the mathematics that is being done in class.

Math demonstrations.   Pairs of students can be stationed in different parts of the classroom, demonstrating interesting math problems they are working on in class. The "mathematician's chair" event, discussed earlier in this chapter, might even be held in conjunction with a curriculum night. Parents would then be able to see children doing mathematics and to talk about the mathematics with the different groups.

Slide show.   Some teachers use cameras to keep records of the year; they may want to show parents slides of the children working on mathematics problems. While this is less immediate than having the children there to demonstrate, it's an easier route to take with younger children. While showing the slides, the teacher explains the mathematics that the children were working on, how they went about it, and what they learned.

Question-and-answer period.   After parents have familiarized themselves with the mathematics in the classroom, they need a chance to raise questions. If they write their questions on index cards, the teacher has a better chance of addressing *all* questions, rather than just those from the most vocal parents. If some questions cannot be addressed adequately during the meeting, the teacher can keep the index card as a reminder and respond in more detail later, perhaps through a letter.

Suggestions for math at home.   Teachers should always be prepared to answer parents' questions about what they can do at home. And if they don't raise questions, we should initiate this discussion ourselves, with suggestions for helping with homework and extending the work that is being done in class. Some parents would welcome a list of books like the one on page 130–131.

Of course, all of this is too much to do in a single parent night. If parents show interest, a second meeting can be held later in the year. And if interest is especially strong, the school may want to sponsor a series of *Family Math* workshops (Stenmark, Thompson, and Cossey, 1986), in which parents and their children come together to do math. Even without the workshops, many parents will enjoy using the *Family Math* activity book with their children at home.

Other good candidates to attend the math curriculum night would be the school principal, the district or school math coordinator, and other teachers. If they already understand the new way of teaching and learning math, they can help articulate it to parents. If they don't, this meeting may be a nonthreatening way for them to learn about it.

Gathering Support for Change

Mathematics needs to be a more pervasive part of students' lives, and the classroom teacher can't make this happen alone. We need to enlist the help of parents, and we need to find support from our colleagues at school. Also, if the teacher's job is ever to become any easier, there must be some outreach to the broader community. Teachers deserve the support of colleagues and administrators in making the changes that are demanded by a constructivist mathematics curriculum. Unfortunately, they may have to create from scratch the support environment that should be there in the first place.

When getting started on this long path, just having the support of one other teacher—someone who can listen to stories about the daily frustrations and perhaps provide a few stories from his or her own classroom—makes a tremendous difference. One or two teachers can gradually transform a school's mathematics culture. Quiet persuasion—by making mathematics visible in classrooms and in the school as a whole—may make a great difference in the long run. Just as a picture is worth a thousand words, the daily pictures of students doing real mathematics go a long way in convincing others of the power of constructivist mathematics.

Books for Parents Interested in Math

Eenie Meenie, Miney Math: Math Play for You and Your Preschooler, by Linda Allison and M. Weston. Boston: Little, Brown, 1993.
This is an especially good resource for parents whose school children have younger (preschool) siblings. It has plenty of suggestions for doing mathematics with everyday routines like cooking and laundry sorting.

Exploring Everyday Math: Ideas for Students, Teachers, and Parents, by Maja Apelman and Julie King. Portsmouth, NH: Heinemann, 1993.
While the primary audience for this comprehensive book is teachers, it provides excellent activities linking home and school mathematics. It also has suggestions for how parents can be involved in their children's mathematics education.

The I Hate Mathematics! Book by Marilyn Burns. Boston: Little, Brown, 1975.
Presented with great humor and lots of cartoon illustrations, this book proves that mathematics is not just arithmetic—and that mathematics can be lots of fun. It offers hundreds of wonderful riddles, magic tricks, experiments, puzzles, games, gags, and things to do that all connect in some way with mathematical reasoning.

Math for Smarty Pants, by Marilyn Burns. Boston: Little, Brown, 1982.
There's more reading in this book than in *The I Hate Mathematics! Book,* but it has a similar humorous tone and similar fascinating puzzles, games, and experiments with number, geometry, and logic, using calculators, calendars, cards,

coins, dice, pencils, and other things you're sure to have around the house. For children who are reluctant readers, parents can read aloud the short (one- and two-page) problem situations.

Helping Your Child Learn Math, by Patsy Kanter. Lexington, MA: D. C. Heath, 1993.
With sponsorship from the U.S. Department of Education, Kanter explains in clear language the goals of the reform movement in mathematics and how these relate to the national education goals for the year 2000. Activities involving math at home are suggested.

Games for Math, by Peggy Kaye. New York: Pantheon Books, 1987.
This book provides lots of easy and fun activities to do at home with kindergarten through third graders.

REFERENCES

Abruscato, Joseph. "Early Results and Tentative Implications from the Vermont Portfolio Project." *Phi Delta Kappan,* February 1993.

Ball, Deborah L. "Unlearning to Teach Mathematics." *For the Learning of Mathematics,* 8, 1988, pp. 40–48.

Burns, Marilyn. *About Teaching Mathematics.* Sausalito, CA: The Math Solution Publications, 1992; distributed by the Cuisenaire Company of America.

Burns, Marilyn. *What Are You Teaching My Child?* New York: Scholastic, 1994. (videotape)

Clements, D. H., M. T. Battista, J. Akers, V. Woolley, J. S. Meredith, and S. McMillen. *Turtle Paths.* A grade 3 unit in *Investigations in Number, Data, and Space.* Palo Alto, CA: Dale Seymour Publications, 1995.

Corwin, Rebecca and May Reinhardt. *Mathematics Education: Learning from the Process Approach to Writing.* Cambridge, MA: Lesley College, 1989.

Corwin, Rebecca B., Susan Jo Russell, and Cornelia Tierney. *Seeing Fractions.* Sacramento: California Department of Education, 1991.

Corwin, Rebecca, et al. *Talking Mathematics: Supporting Classroom Discourse.* Portsmouth, NH: Heinemann, 1995.

Countryman, Joan. *Writing to Learn Mathematics: Strategies That Work,* K–12. Portsmouth, NH: Heinemann, 1992.

Daro, Phillip. *A Framework for Balance.* Oakland, CA: The New Standards Project, 1993.

Davis, Philip J. and Reuben Hersh. *The Mathematical Experience.* Boston: Birkhauser, 1981.

Dewdney, A. K. *200% of Nothing.* New York: Wiley, 1993.

Duckworth, Eleanor. *The Having of Wonderful Ideas and Other Essays on Teaching and Learning.* New York: Teachers College Press, 1987.

Fennema, E., T. Carpenter, and P. Peterson. "Learning Mathematics with Understanding: Cognitively Guided Instruction." *Advances in Research on Teaching,* 1, 1989, pp. 195–221.

Gray, Eddie M. and David Tall. "Duality, Ambiguity, and Flexibility: A 'Proceptual' View of Arithmetic." *Journal of Research in Mathematics Education,* 2(2), 1994, pp. 116–140.

Hart, Diane. *Authentic Assessment: A Handbook for Educators.* Menlo Park, CA: Addison-Wesley, 1994.

Hembree, R. and D. Dessart. "Effects of Hand-held Calculator in Precollege Mathematics Education: A Meta-analysis." *Journal for Research in Mathematics Education,* 17(2), 1986, pp. 83–89.

Hirsch, E. D., Jr. *Cultural Literacy: What Every American Needs to Know.* Boston: Houghton Mifflin, 1987.

Kamii, Constance, ed. *Achievement Testing in the Early Grades: The Games Grown-Ups Play.* Washington, DC: National Association for the Education of Young Children, 1990.

Kamii, Constance, and Barbara A. Lewis. "The Harmful Effects of Algorithms in Primary Arithmetic." *Teaching K–8,* January 1993, pp. 36–38.

Kamii, Constance, Barbara A. Lewis, and Sally Jones Livingston. "Primary Arithmetic: Children Inventing Their Own Procedures." *Arithmetic Teacher,* December 1993.

Kaye, Peggy. *Games for Math,* New York: Pantheon Books, 1987.

Leinwand, Steven. "It's Time to Abandon Computational Algorithms." *Education Week,* February 9, 1994.

MacNeal, Edward. *Mathsemantics: Making Numbers Talk Sense.* New York: Viking, 1994.

Math Matters: Kids Are Counting on You. Chicago: The National PTA, 1989. (videotape and materials package)

Mitchell, Ruth. *Testing for Learning: How New Approaches to Evaluation Can Improve American Schools.* New York: The Free Press, 1992.

Mumme, Judy. *Portfolio Assessment in Mathematics.* California Mathematics Project, University of California, Santa Barbara, 1990.

National Center for Fair and Open Testing. *Standardized Tests and Our Children: A Guide to Testing Reform.* Cambridge, MA: National Center for Fair and Open Testing, 1991.

National Council of Teachers of Mathematics. *Curriculum and Evaluation Standards for School Mathematics.* Reston, VA: NCTM, 1989.

National Council of Teachers of Mathematics. *Professional Standards for Teaching Mathematics.* Reston, VA: NCTM, 1991.

National Council of Teachers of Mathematics. *Assessment Standards for School Mathematics.* Reston, VA: NCTM, 1995.

National Research Council. *Everybody Counts.* Washington, DC: National Academy Press, 1989.

Nemirovsky, Ricardo. "Rethinking Calculus Education." *Hands On!* 16(1), p. 1, 14–17. Cambridge, MA: TERC, 1993.

Ohanian, Susan. *Garbage Pizza, Patchwork Quilts, and Math Magic: Stories About Teachers Who Love to Teach and Children Who Love to Learn.* New York: W. H. Freeman, 1992.

Parker, Ruth. *Mathematical Power: Lessons from a Classroom.* Portsmouth, NH: Heinemann, 1993.

Paulos, John A. *Innumeracy.* New York: Hill & Wang, 1988.

Perrone, Vito, ed. *Expanding Student Assessment.* Alexandria, VA: Association for Supervision and Curriculum Development, 1991.

Piaget, J. and A. Szeminska. *The Child's Conception of Number.* New York: Norton, 1965. (Original work published in 1941.)

Piaget, J. and R. Garcia. *Understanding Causality.* New York: Norton, 1974.

Prisoners of Time. Report of the National Education Commission on Time and Learning. Washington, DC: U.S. Government Printing Office, 1994.

Romangnano, Lew. *Wrestling with Change.* Portsmouth, NH: Heinemann, 1994.

Russell, Susan Jo, Rebecca B. Corwin, Susan J. Friel, Jan Mokros, and Antonia Stone. *Used Numbers: Real Data in the Classroom.* Palo Alto, CA: Dale Seymour Publications, 1990.

Russell, Susan Jo and Andee Rubin. *Landmarks in the Hundreds.* A grade 3 unit in *Investigations in Number, Data, and Space.* Palo Alto, CA: Dale Seymour Publications, 1995.

Russell, Susan Jo, Cornelia C. Tierney, Jan Mokros, et al. *Investigations in Number, Data, and Space.* Palo Alto, CA: Dale Seymour Publications, 1995 and in press. A K–5 mathematics curriculum from TERC, with a set of units at each grade level.

Schifter, Deborah, and Catherine T. Fosnot. *Restructuring Mathematics Education: Stories of Teachers Meeting the Challenge of Reform.* New York: Teachers College Press, 1993.

Schwartz, Judah. "The Intellectual Prices of Secrecy in Mathematics Assessment." In R. Lesh & S. J. Lamon (eds.), *Assessment of Authentic Performance in School Mathematics.* Washington, DC: American Association for the Advancement of Science, 1992.

Seeing and Thinking Mathematically. Glenn Kleiman, Principal Investigator. Education Development Center, 55 Chapel Street, Newton, MA 02160. "The Language of Number" (1994) for 6th and 7th grade available from Heinemann, Portsmouth, NH.

Simon, Martin. "Prospective Elementary Teachers' Knowledge of Division." *Journal of Research in Mathematics Education,* 24(3), 1993, pp. 233–254.

Stenmark, Jean Kerr. *Assessment Alternatives in Mathematics.* Berkeley, CA: EQUALS, University of California, 1989.

Stenmark, Jean, Virginia Thompson, and Ruth Cossey. *Family Math.* Berkeley, CA: Lawrence Hall of Science, University of California, 1986.

Stevenson, Harold, and James W. Stigler. *The Learning Gap: Why Our Schools Are Failing and What We Can Learn from Japanese and Chinese Education.* New York: Simon & Schuster, 1992.

Stevenson, Harold, S-Y Lee, and J. W. Stigler. "Mathematics Achievement of Chinese, Japanese, and American Children." *Science,* 231, 1986, pp. 693–699.

Suydam, Marilyn. "An Overview of Research: Computers in Mathematics Education K–12." *Mathematics Education Digest,* No. 1, ERIC Clearinghouse for Science, Mathematics, and Environmental Education. Columbus, OH: Ohio State University, 1986.

The Connected Mathematics Project. Jim Fey and Glenda Lappan, Principal Investigators. 101 Willis House, Michigan State University, East Lansing, MI 48824.

Tierney, Cornelia and Ricardo Nemirovsky. "Children's Spontaneous Representations of Changing Situations." *Hands On!* 14(2), pp. 7–10, Cambridge, MA: TERC, 1991.

U.S. Department of Education, National Assessment of Educational Progress. *NAEP 1992 Trends in Academic Progress.* Washington, DC: NAEP, 1994.

Wheelock, Anne. *Crossing the Tracks: How Untracking Can Save America's Schools.* New York: The New Press, 1992.